Practical Internet of Things with JavaScript

Build standalone exciting IoT projects with Raspberry Pi 3 and JavaScript (ES5/ES6)

Arvind Ravulavaru

BIRMINGHAM - MUMBAI

Practical Internet of Things with JavaScript

First published: December 2017

Production reference: 1211217

Published by Packt Publishing Ltd.
Livery Place
35 Livery Street
Birmingham
B3 2PB, UK.

ISBN 978-1-78829-294-8

www.packtpub.com

Credits

Authors
Arvind Ravulavaru

Reviewers
Vijaya Kumar Suda

Commissioning Editor
Vijin Boricha

Acquisition Editor
Reshma Raman

Content Development Editor
Eisha Dsouza

Technical Editor
Varsha Shivhare

Copy Editor
Safis Editing

Project Coordinator
Kinjal Bari

Proofreader
Safis Editing

Indexer
Pratik Shirodkar

Graphics
Kirk D'Penha

Production Coordinator
Shantanu Zagade

About the Author

Arvind Ravulavaru is a platform architect at Ubiconn IoT Solutions, with over 9 years of experience in software development and 2 years in hardware and product development. For the last 5 years, he has been working extensively on JavaScript, both on the server side and the client side, and for the last couple of years in IoT, building a platform for rapidly developing IoT solutions, named the IoT Suitcase. Prior to this, he has worked on big data, cloud computing, and orchestration.

Arvind has already written couple of books named *Learning Ionic* and *Learning Ionic - Second Edition*, which talks about building Mobile Hybrid applications using Ionic framework v1, v2, and v3.

First off, I would like to thank all the people who have purchased my Learning Ionic and Learning Ionic second edition books. The support from you guys has been tremendous. I really appreciate it. I would like to thank the Packt team for doing an amazing job in releasing and promoting the book. A very special thanks to my 4-month-old lab, Dexter for letting me write my book without bothering much to play with him at nights. Thanks to the team at Ubiconn IoT Solutions who were behind me in getting this book out. Special thanks to Ramesh Noothi, for helping me set up the hardware as well Nagesh Adicharla, who has also created all the schematic images for the book.

Last but not the least, thanks to the entire team at Packt for supporting me. I sincerely thank my content development editor, Eisha Dsouza and technical editor, Varsha Shivhare for their awesome support. Thanks to Reshma Raman and the production team for taking the book to press. Special thanks to my family, without whose support this book wouldn't have been possible. Thank you.

About the Reviewer

Vijay Suda has over 17 years of experience in the IT industry. He works as a solution architect for a major consulting firm in the USA, operating in the Java, cloud, IoT, big data, and machine learning spaces. He worked for Tata Consultancy Services and Wipro Technologies in solution architecture, design and development of enterprise level systems with Java/J2EE, and SOA-related technologies. He has experience with various clients in the banking, telecom, and retail domains in Switzerland, Belgium, Mexico, Bahrain, India, and the USA.

He is passionate about implementing AI and machine learning algorithms to make a positive impact on society. He has recently been working on deep learning technologies such as TensorFlow, scikit-learn, and pandas for machine learning.

I would like to thank my father, Koteswara Rao Suda, and my mother, Rajyalakshmi Suda, for watching my first steps and supporting me in every step to reach here; my dear wife Radhika for everything she has done for me; my lovely son Chandra; and my cute daughter Akshaya for her warming smile.

www.PacktPub.com

For support files and downloads related to your book, please visit www.PacktPub.com.

Did you know that Packt offers eBook versions of every book published, with PDF and ePub files available? You can upgrade to the eBook version at www.PacktPub.com and as a print book customer, you are entitled to a discount on the eBook copy. Get in touch with us at service@packtpub.com for more details.

At www.PacktPub.com, you can also read a collection of free technical articles, sign up for a range of free newsletters and receive exclusive discounts and offers on Packt books and eBooks.

https://www.packtpub.com/mapt

Get the most in-demand software skills with Mapt. Mapt gives you full access to all Packt books and video courses, as well as industry-leading tools to help you plan your personal development and advance your career.

Why subscribe?

- Fully searchable across every book published by Packt
- Copy and paste, print, and bookmark content
- On demand and accessible via a web browser

Customer Feedback

Thanks for purchasing this Packt book. At Packt, quality is at the heart of our editorial process. To help us improve, please leave us an honest review on this book's Amazon page at `https://www.amazon.com/dp/1788292944`.

If you'd like to join our team of regular reviewers, you can email us at `customerreviews@packtpub.com`. We award our regular reviewers with free eBooks and videos in exchange for their valuable feedback. Help us be relentless in improving our products!

Fear lies in the unknown

Table of Contents

Preface

We are part of a generation where people have already started adapting to IoT products. There is a lot of hype about IoT. This book will focus on building IoT-based applications that will help you to achieve a higher level of understanding when it comes to IoT. It will follow a project-based approach that will teach you to build standalone exciting, applications and will also teach you to extend your project to another level. We are going to use JavaScript as our programming language and Raspberry Pi 3 as our hardware to build interesting IoT solutions.

What this book covers

Chapter 1, *The World of IoT*, introduces you to the world of IoT. We will be looking at the history of IoT, identifying a few use cases, and getting a technical overview of what were are going to cover in this book.

Chapter 2, *IoTFW.js - I*, walks you through how to build a reference framework for developing IoT solutions using JavaScript. In this chapter, we cover the high-level architecture and get started with installing the required software. We will start with downloading the base application and stitching the Raspberry Pi together with the MQTTS broker and API engine.

Chapter 3, *IoTFW.js - II*, continues from where we left off in the previous chapter and completes the implementation of the API engine, web app, desktop app, and mobile app. At the end of this chapter, we implement a simple example with an LED and a temperature sensor, where instructions from the apps will turn the LED on/off and the value of the temperature sensor updates in real time.

Chapter 4, *Smart Agriculture*, talks about building a simple weather station using the reference architecture we have built. The weather station consists of four sensors, and using these we can monitor farm conditions. We will be making the required changes to the API engine, web app, desktop app, and mobile app.

Chapter 5, *Smart Agriculture and Voice AI*, shows how we can leverage the power of voice AI technology to build interesting IoT solutions. We are going to work with the smart weather station and add a one-channel mechanical relay to this setup. Then, using voice commands and Amazon Alexa, we are going to manage the weather station.

Chapter 6, *Smart Wearable*, talks about an interesting use case in the healthcare sector, postoperation patient care. Using a smart wearable device equipped with a simple accelerometer, one can easily detect whether a patient has fallen down. In this chapter, we build the required setup comment to gather the accelerometer values from the sensor.

Chapter 7, *Smart Wearable and IFTTT*, explains how the data collected from the accelerometer can be used to detect falls and at the same time notify the API engine. Using a popular concept named **If This Then That** (**IFTTT**)—we will be building our own rules engine, which will process predefined rules and take action accordingly. In our example, we are going to send an email to the patient's carer if a fall is detected.

Chapter 8, *Raspberry Pi Image Streaming*, shows how to take advantage of the Raspberry Pi camera module to build a real-time image streaming (MJPEG technology) solution to monitor your surroundings from anywhere in the world. We will also implement motion-based video capture to capture video when motion is detected.

Chapter 9, *Smart Surveillance*, walks you through the process of image recognition using Amazon's Rekognition platform. We will be capturing an image when motion is detected using the Raspberry Pi 3 camera module. Then, we will send this image to Amazon Rekognition platform to detect whether the image we have taken is of an intruder or of someone we know.

What you need for this book

To start building IoT solutions using JavaScript, you need to have the following:

- Medium to advanced knowledge of JavaScript – ES5 and ES6
- Medium to advanced knowledge of MEAN stack application development
- Medium to advanced knowledge of Angular 4
- Medium to advanced knowledge of Electron Framework
- Medium to advanced knowledge of Ionic Framework 3
- Novice to medium knowledge of digital electronic circuits
- Novice to medium knowledge of Raspberry Pi
- Novice to medium knowledge on sensors and actuators

Who this book is for

It is for readers who are already well versed with JavaScript and want to extend their JavaScript knowledge to building hardware solutions in the field of IoT. IoT enthusiasts interested in creating exciting projects will also find this book useful. This book is also useful for readers who are good at developing standalone solutions using Raspberry Pi; this book will help them add IoT capabilities to their existing projects using the world's most misunderstood programming language.

Conventions

In this book, you will find a number of text styles that distinguish between different kinds of information. Here are some examples of these styles and an explanation of their meaning. Code words in text, database table names, folder names, filenames, file extensions, pathnames, dummy URLs, user input, and Twitter handles are shown as follows: "Now, inside the broker folder, create another folder named certs and cd into that folder." A block of code is set as follows:

```
// MongoDB connection options
    mongo: {
        uri: 'mongodb://admin:admin123@ds241055.mlab.com:41055/iotfwjs'
    },

    mqtt: {
        host: process.env.EMQTT_HOST || '127.0.0.1',
        clientId: 'API_Server_Dev',
        port: 8883
    }
};
```

Any command-line input or output is written as follows:

```
openssl req -newkey rsa:2048 -nodes -keyout key.pem -x509 -days 365 -out
certificate.pem
```

New terms and **important words** are shown in bold. Words that you see on the screen, for example, in menus or dialog boxes, appear in the text like this: "Once logged in, click on the **Create New** button to create a new DB."

Warnings or important notes appear like this.

 Tips and tricks appear like this.

Reader feedback

Feedback from our readers is always welcome. Let us know what you think about this book-what you liked or disliked. Reader feedback is important for us as it helps us develop titles that you will really get the most out of. To send us general feedback, simply email feedback@packtpub.com, and mention the book's title in the subject of your message. If there is a topic that you have expertise in and you are interested in either writing or contributing to a book, see our author guide at www.packtpub.com/authors.

Customer support

Now that you are the proud owner of a Packt book, we have a number of things to help you to get the most from your purchase.

Downloading the example code

You can download the example code files for this book from your account at http://www.packtpub.com. If you purchased this book elsewhere, you can visit http://www.packtpub.com/support and register to have the files emailed directly to you. You can download the code files by following these steps:

1. Log in or register to our website using your email address and password.
2. Hover the mouse pointer on the **SUPPORT** tab at the top.
3. Click on **Code Downloads & Errata**.
4. Enter the name of the book in the **Search** box.
5. Select the book for which you're looking to download the code files.
6. Choose from the drop-down menu where you purchased this book from.
7. Click on **Code Download**.

Once the file is downloaded, please make sure that you unzip or extract the folder using the latest version of:

- WinRAR / 7-Zip for Windows
- Zipeg / iZip / UnRarX for Mac
- 7-Zip / PeaZip for Linux

The code bundle for the book is also hosted on GitHub at
`https://github.com/PacktPublishing/Practical-Internet-of-Things-with-JavaScript`. We also have other code bundles from our rich catalog of books and videos available at `https://github.com/PacktPublishing/`. Check them out!

Downloading the color images of this book

We also provide you with a PDF file that has color images of the screenshots/diagrams used in this book. The color images will help you better understand the changes in the output. You can download this file from `https://www.packtpub.com/sites/default/files/downloads/PracticalInternetofThingswithJavaScript_ColorImages.pdf`.

Errata

Although we have taken every care to ensure the accuracy of our content, mistakes do happen. If you find a mistake in one of our books-maybe a mistake in the text or the code- we would be grateful if you could report this to us. By doing so, you can save other readers from frustration and help us improve subsequent versions of this book. If you find any errata, please report them by visiting `http://www.packtpub.com/submit-errata`, selecting your book, clicking on the **Errata Submission Form** link, and entering the details of your errata. Once your errata are verified, your submission will be accepted and the errata will be uploaded to our website or added to any list of existing errata under the Errata section of that title. To view the previously submitted errata, go to `https://www.packtpub.com/books/content/support` and enter the name of the book in the search field. The required information will appear under the **Errata** section.

Piracy

Piracy of copyrighted material on the internet is an ongoing problem across all media. At Packt, we take the protection of our copyright and licenses very seriously. If you come across any illegal copies of our works in any form on the internet, please provide us with the location address or website name immediately so that we can pursue a remedy. Please contact us at copyright@packtpub.com with a link to the suspected pirated material. We appreciate your help in protecting our authors and our ability to bring you valuable content.

Questions

If you have a problem with any aspect of this book, you can contact us at questions@packtpub.com, and we will do our best to address the problem.

1
The World of IoT

Welcome to advanced IoT with JavaScript. In this book, we will look at building IoT solutions using JavaScript as our programming language. Before we start with the technical deep dive, I would like to talk about the world of IoT, the solutions offered by it, and what responsibilities fall on bestows on us developers who make these products. In this chapter, we will look at the following topics:

- The world of IoT
- History of IoT
- IoT uses cases
- Technology overview
- Product engineering

The world of IoT

Imagine a scenario where you have run out of milk; you have noticed it and put it on your shopping list. But due to unforeseen reasons, you forgot to buy milk; well, you don't have milk for the next day.

Now imagine another scenario: you have a smart fridge, and it noticed that you are running out of milk, puts milk on your shopping list, and then updates your GPS route to come home via the supermarket, but you still forget it.

You have to now face the wrath of your refrigerator.

Now that things are getting real, imagine another situation where your fridge has skipped the middleman, you, and now directly places an order on Amazon, and Amazon delivers it by the time you need your breakfast the next day.

Scenario three is what is we are after. Let one machine talk to another machine and take decisions accordingly; things such as the type of milk, quantity, and expiry date are automatically validated before purchase.

We humans are now using the world of connected devices and smart devices to make our lives better.

What is IoT?

If you have been breathing for at least a decade, you must have heard terms such as smart living, smart spaces, and intelligent devices. All these refer to a parent concept called the **Internet of Things (IoT)**.

In simple words, IoT is when we have our electronic, electrical, or electro-mechanical devices connect to the internet and talk to each other.

Smart devices primarily revolve around two things:

- Sensors
- Actuators

Any solution in the IoT space is either sensing something or actuating something.

With this technology, we have found the solution for Sheldon Cooper (from the Big Bang theory, CBS TV series), where he wants to know who sits on his spot as soon as someone sits on it:

Source: http://bigbangtheory.wikia.com/wiki/Sheldon%27s_Spot

All we do is place a weight sensor underneath the cushion, and if the weight increases, the sensor will trigger the camera pointing at the sofa to take a picture and send a push notification to him with the picture. How about that?

I know I have pushed the examples a bit, but you get the point, right?

A bit of history

IoT has existed in various forms for more than 35 years. The earliest example I found was a Coke machine at Carnegie Mellon University in 1982. Developed by four graduate students, Mike Kazar, David Nichols, John Zsarnay, and Ivor Durham, they hooked up the Coke machine to the internet so that they could check from their desks whether the machine was loaded with cold Coke. Source (`https://www.cs.cmu.edu/~coke/`).

Sir Timothy John Berners-Lee invented the first webpage in 1991.

Another example is the internet toaster by John Romkey. He connected his toaster to the internet using the TCP/IP protocol. He created one control to turn on the toaster and one control to turn it off. Of course, someone had to put the bread in the toaster:

Source: http://ieeexplore.ieee.org/document/7786805/

Another interesting IoT example is the Trojan Room coffee pot. This was created by Quentin Stafford-Fraser and Paul Jardetzky in 1993. A camera was located in the Trojan Room in the computer laboratory of the University of Cambridge. It monitored the coffee pot levels, with an image being updated about three times a minute and sent to the building's server:

Source: https://en.wikipedia.org/wiki/Trojan_Room_coffee_pot

As mentioned previously, we can see that even before we could imagine the possibilities, people had already worked on internet-related solutions.

Over the past 2 years, there was one thing that I kept on seeing and started believing strongly:

> *"Laziness is the mother of Invention."*

Not necessity, not boredom, but laziness. In this day and age, nobody wants to do mundane things such as grocery shopping, walking up to a switch, and turning on a light or AC. So, we are searching for new and innovative ways to solve these problems.

IoT use cases

Now that you have a feel for IoT, you can imagine the literally infinite possibilities that can be built using this piece of technology.

Based on my observations, IoT use cases can be crudely classified into three parts:

- Problem solving
- Convenience
- Showing off

The problem solving part comes in where IoT is used to solve a real-world problem, for instance, a farmer whose farm is located half a kilometre from their home, and they have to walk all the way to the farm to turn on their water pumps/motors . Another scenario is where a post-operation patient's vital statistics can be sent to the hospital periodically after his/her discharge, to monitor the patient for any abnormalities. This is where IoT fits in pretty well.

Convenience is where you can turn on your air conditioner 30 mins before you reach your home so you can chill as you enter or unlock your door from your work if someone you know knocks at your door and you are not nearby.

showing off is where you go to another country just to turn on or off your porch light, just to show that IoT works.

All of them are forms of consumption of this technology.

In this book, we will look at covering a few solutions that fall into previous use cases.

Technology overview

Now that we know what IoT is, we can start defining the technology stack. In this book, we will build a generic framework using JavaScript for developing IoT applications.

We will follow the approach of cloud computing, where we have a bunch of devices that are connected to the cloud, compared to a fog computing approach, where there is a gateway that can do almost all the things a cloud can but is locally available in the on-premises.

Our smart devices will be powered by Raspberry Pi 3, which has the ability to talk to the cloud over Wi-Fi and also, using its GPIO pins, talk to the sensors and actuators. Using this simple piece of hardware, we will connect sensors and actuators and build some real-world solutions in this book.

Another alternative to Raspberry Pi 3 is Raspberry Pi Zero W, which is a miniature version of Raspberry Pi 3, in case you are looking to build a compact solution.

We will walk through each piece of technology in Chapter 2, *IoTFW.js - I* and Chapter 3, *IoTFW.js - II,* and from there on use these technologies to build IoT solutions in various domains.

Product engineering

Unlike software development, hardware development is well hard. The time taken, the complexity, and the execution are expensive. Imagine a syntax error in a JavaScript console; all we need to do is go to the specific line number, make the changes, and then refresh the browser.

Now compare this with hardware product development. From the time a piece of hardware is identified to when it is put on a supermarket shelf as a shrink-wrapped product takes at least 8 months, with at least four iterations of the product being made to validate and test it in the real world.

To give another example, the positioning of components on a product makes or breaks it. Imagine if there were no ridges or grip on a charger plug; your hand will always slip while pulling the charger out of the socket. This is value engineering.

Putting together a **Proof Of Concept** (**POC**) is very simple, as you will see in the rest of this book. Turning this POC into a shrink-wrapped product is a different ball game altogether. The difference is the same as between singing in your bathroom and singing on a stage with millions of people watching you.

Remember that the examples that we will build in this book are all POCs, and none of them are remotely close to being used in the production of a product. You can always use the solutions we will work on in this book to gain a better understanding of implementation and then design your own solution around them.

Summary

In this chapter, we looked at what IoT is and a bit of history about it. Next, we saw a couple of use cases, a high-level technology overview, and a bit about product engineering.

In Chapter 2, *IoTFW.js - I,* we will get started with building the IoT framework on which we will build our solutions.

2
IoTFW.js - I

In this chapter and `Chapter 3`, *IoTFW.js - II*, we are going to develop a reference architecture for building various IoT solutions. The reference architecture or the IoT framework will be serving as a base for our future IoT solutions that we are going to be working on in this book. We will be calling this reference architecture or framework as IoTFW.js. We will be working on the following topics to bring IoTFW.js to life:

- Designing an IoTFW.js architecture
- Developing a Node.js based server-side layer
- Developing an Angular 4 based web app
- Developing an Ionic 3 based mobile app
- Developing an Angular 4 and Electron.js desktop app
- Setting up and installing the required dependencies on a Raspberry Pi 3
- Integrating all the pieces

We are going to cover some of the previous topics in this chapter and some in `Chapter 3`, *IoTFW.js - II*.

Designing a reference architecture

As we have seen in `Chapter 1`, *The World of IoT*, all the examples we are going to work on have a common setup. That would be the hardware, firmware (software running on the hardware), broker, API engine and the user apps.

We will be expanding on the relevant pieces of framework as we come across it.

As and when we need to, we will be expanding on the hardware, or mobile app, or the API engine.

With this reference architecture, we are going to establish a pipeline between the devices present in the real world to the cloud in the virtual world. In other words, IoT is a last mile solution between devices and the internet.

Architecture

A simple reference architecture with Raspberry Pi, Wi-Fi gateway, the cloud engine, and the user interface apps stitched together would look as shown in the following diagram:

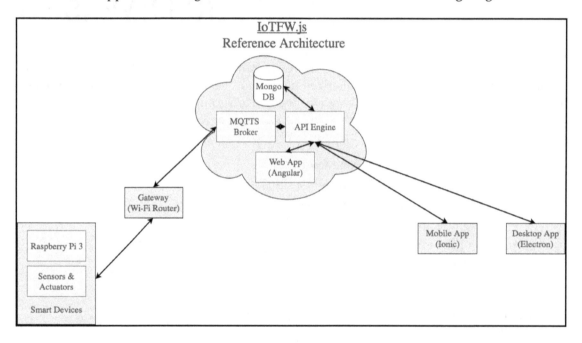

At a very high level, we have smart devices on the left-hand side and the user devices on the right-hand side. All of the communication between them happens through the cloud.

Following is a description of each key entity in the previous architecture. We are going to start from the left-hand side and move towards the right.

Smart device

Smart devices are hardware entities that consist of a sensor, or actuator, or both, any micro controller or micro processor, in our case, a Raspberry pi 3.

A sensor is an electronic component that can sense or measure a physical property and relay it back to a microcontroller or a microprocessor. The data relayed back can be periodic or event-driven; event-driven as in when there is change in data only. A temperature sensor such as an LM35 or DHT11 is an example of a sensor.

An actuator is also an electro-mechanical component that can trigger actions in the real world. Generally, the actuators do not act by themselves. A microcontroller, a microprocessor, or an electronic logic sends signals to the actuator. An example of an actuator is a mechanical relay.

The micro-processor we were referring would be a Raspberry Pi 3 for this book.

The Raspberry Pi 3 is a single-board computer, designed and developed by the Raspberry Pi foundation. The Raspberry Pi 3 is the third-generation Raspberry Pi.

In this book, we are going to use a Raspberry Pi 3 model B for all the examples. Some of the specifications of the Raspberry Pi 3 model B are as follows:

Feature	Specification
Generation	3
Release date	February 2016
Architecture	ARMv8-A (64/32-bit)
System on a Chip (SoC)	Broadcom BCM2837
CPU	1.2 GHz 64-bit quad-core ARM Cortex-A53
Memory (SDRAM)	1 GB (shared with GPU)
USB 2.0 ports	4 (via the on-board 5-port USB hub)
On-board network	10/100 Mbit/s Ethernet, 802.11n wireless, Bluetooth 4.1
Low-level peripherals	17× GPIO plus the same specific functions, and HAT ID bus
Power ratings	300 mA (1.5 W) average when idle, 1.34 A (6.7 W) maximum under stress (monitor, keyboard, mouse, and Wi-Fi connected)
Power source	5 V via MicroUSB or GPIO header

For more information on the specifications, please refer to the specifications of Raspberry Pi:
https://en.wikipedia.org/wiki/Raspberry_Pi#Specifications.

Gateway

The next piece in our architecture is the Wi-Fi router. A common household Wi-Fi router will act as a gateway for us. As we have seen in Chapter 1, *The World of IoT*, in the *Clustered devices versus standalone devices* section, we are following the approach of standalone devices, where each device is self-sufficient and has a radio of its own to communicate with the outside world. All the projects we are going to build consist of a Raspberry Pi 3, which has a microprocessor as well as the radio to interface with the sensors, and actuators with the internet.

MQTTS broker

The next important piece in our reference framework is the secure communication channel between the device and the cloud. We are going to use MQTT as our communication channel. MQTT is described in the following quote from http://mqtt.org/faq:

> *MQTT stands for MQ Telemetry Transport. It is a publish/subscribe, extremely simple and lightweight messaging protocol, designed for constrained devices and low-bandwidth, high-latency or unreliable networks. The design principles are to minimise network bandwidth and device resource requirements whilst also attempting to ensure reliability and some degree of assurance of delivery.*

We are going to use the MQTT over SSL or MQTTS. In our architecture, we are going to use Mosca (http://www.mosca.io/) as our MQTTS broker. Mosca is a Node.js MQTT broker. We will talk more about Mosca when we start working with it.

API engine

An API engine is a web server application, written on Node.js, Express with persistence layer as MongoDB. This engine is responsible for communicating with Mosca as a MQTT client, persisting data into MongoDB as well as to expose APIs using Express. These APIs are then consumed by the apps to display the data.

We will also be implementing a socket-based API for user interfaces to get notified in real time from the devices between the apps and the server.

MongoDB

We are going to use MongoDB as our data persistence layer. MongoDB is a NoSQL document database that allows us to save documents with different schemas in one collection. This kind of database is well suited for dealing with sensor data from various devices, as the data structure or the parameters vary from solution to solution. To know more about MongoDB, refer to `https://www.mongodb.com/`.

Web app

The web app is a simple web/mobile web interface, which will implement the APIs exposed by the API engine. These APIs will include authentication, access a particular smart device, get the latest data from the smart device, and send data back to the smart device over APIs. We are going to use Angular 4 (`https://angular.io/`) and Twitter Bootstrap 3 (`http://getbootstrap.com/`) technologies to build the web app.

Mobile app

We are going to follow a mobile hybrid approach for building our mobile app. The mobile app implements the APIs exposed by the API engine. These APIs will include authentication, access a particular smart device, get the latest data from the smart device and send data back to the smart device over APIs. We are going to use Ionic 3 (`http://ionicframework.com/`), which is powered by Angular 4, to build the mobile app.

Desktop app

We are going to follow a desktop hybrid approach for building our desktop app. The desktop app will implement the APIs exposed by the API engine. These APIs will include authentication, access a particular smart device, get the latest data from the smart device, and send data back to the smart device over APIs. We are going to use Electron (`https://electron.atom.io/`) as the shell for building the desktop app. We will be using Angular 4 and Twitter Bootstrap 3 (`http://getbootstrap.com/`) technologies to build the desktop app. We try and reuse as much code as possible between the web and desktop apps.

Data flow

Now that we have an understanding of the various pieces of the architecture, we will now look at the data flow between the components. We are going to talk about the data flow from the smart device to the apps and vice versa.

Smart device to the apps

A simple flow of data from a sensor to a user device will be as follows:

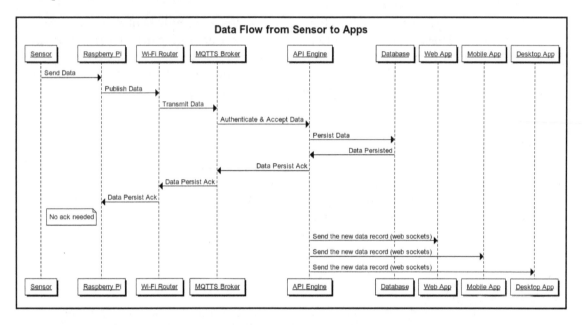

As you can see from the previous figure, the data originates at the sensor; this data is read by the Raspberry Pi 3 and published to the MQTTS broker (Mosca) via the Wi-Fi router. Once the broker receives the data, it will send the same to the API engine, which will persist the data to the DB. Once the data has been successfully saved, the API engine will send the new data to our app, to show the data in real time.

An important thing to notice here is that the API engine will act as an MQTT client and subscribe to topics on which the device publishes the data. We will look at these topics when we go over the implementation.

Generally, the data in this flow would be a typical sensor transmitting data.

App to the smart device

The following diagram shows how the data flows from an app to the smart device:

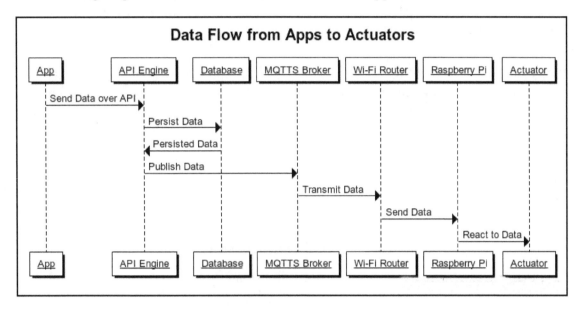

As we can see from the previous diagram, if the app wishes to send an instruction to the smart device, it sends that message to the API engine. The API engine then persists that data into the database and publishes the same to the MQTTS broker, to be passed on to the device. The device then reacts to that data on the actuator.

Do note that in both the flows, the MQTTS broker manages the devices and the API engine manages the apps.

Building the reference architecture

In this section, we are going to start putting together all the pieces and stitch together the required setup. We are going to start with Node.js installation, then the database, and after that, move on to other pieces.

Installing Node.js on the server

Before we continue with our development, we need Node.js on our server. The server here could be your own desktop, laptop, an AWS machine, or a digitalocean instance, which may or may not have a public IP
(https://www.iplocation.net/public-vs-private-ip-address).

To install Node.js, navigate to https://nodejs.org/en/ and download the appropriate version for your machine. Once installation is completed, you can test the installation by running the from a command prompt/terminal:

```
node -v
# v6.10.1
```

and

```
npm -v
# 3.10.10
```

You may have a later version than the one shown previously.

Now that we have the required software, we will continue.

Installing nodemon

Now that we have Node.js installed, we will install nodemon. This will take care of auto restarting our node application. Run:

```
npm install -g nodemon
```

MongoDB

You can follow one of the following two ways listed to set up the database.

Local installation

We can set up MongoDB on our server as a stand-alone installation. This way, the DB is running on the server and the data is persisted there.

Depending on your OS, you can follow the instructions provided at
`https://docs.mongodb.com/manual/installation/` to set up the database.

Once you have installed the DB, to test whether everything is working fine, you can open a
new terminal and start the Mongo daemon by running the following:

mongod

You should see something similar to the following:

```
→  ~ mongod
2017-04-29T17:31:59.986+0530 I CONTROL  [initandlisten] MongoDB starting : pid=27884 port=27017 dbpath=/data
/db 64-bit host=Arvinds-MacBook-Pro.local
2017-04-29T17:31:59.987+0530 I CONTROL  [initandlisten] db version v3.4.2
2017-04-29T17:31:59.987+0530 I CONTROL  [initandlisten] git version: 3f76e40c105fc223b3e5aac3e20dcd026b83b38
b
2017-04-29T17:31:59.987+0530 I CONTROL  [initandlisten] OpenSSL version: OpenSSL 1.0.2k  26 Jan 2017
2017-04-29T17:31:59.987+0530 I CONTROL  [initandlisten] allocator: system
2017-04-29T17:31:59.987+0530 I CONTROL  [initandlisten] modules: none
2017-04-29T17:31:59.987+0530 I CONTROL  [initandlisten] build environment:
2017-04-29T17:31:59.987+0530 I CONTROL  [initandlisten]     distarch: x86_64
2017-04-29T17:31:59.987+0530 I CONTROL  [initandlisten]     target_arch: x86_64
2017-04-29T17:31:59.987+0530 I CONTROL  [initandlisten] options: {}
2017-04-29T17:31:59.987+0530 I -        [initandlisten] Detected data files in /data/db created by the 'mmap
v1' storage engine, so setting the active storage engine to 'mmapv1'.
2017-04-29T17:31:59.997+0530 I JOURNAL  [initandlisten] journal dir=/data/db/journal
2017-04-29T17:31:59.997+0530 I JOURNAL  [initandlisten] recover : no journal files present, no recovery need
ed
2017-04-29T17:32:00.013+0530 I JOURNAL  [durability] Durability thread started
2017-04-29T17:32:00.013+0530 I JOURNAL  [journal writer] Journal writer thread started
2017-04-29T17:32:00.013+0530 I CONTROL  [initandlisten]
2017-04-29T17:32:00.013+0530 I CONTROL  [initandlisten] ** WARNING: Access control is not enabled for the da
tabase.
2017-04-29T17:32:00.013+0530 I CONTROL  [initandlisten] **          Read and write access to data and config
uration is unrestricted.
2017-04-29T17:32:00.013+0530 I CONTROL  [initandlisten]
2017-04-29T17:32:00.013+0530 I CONTROL  [initandlisten]
2017-04-29T17:32:00.013+0530 I CONTROL  [initandlisten] ** WARNING: soft rlimits too low. Number of files is
 256, should be at least 1000
2017-04-29T17:32:00.197+0530 I FTDC     [initandlisten] Initializing full-time diagnostic data capture with
directory '/data/db/diagnostic.data'
2017-04-29T17:32:00.205+0530 I NETWORK  [thread1] waiting for connections on port 27017
```

I am running the database on the default port `27017`.

Now we will interact with the database using the mongo shell. Open a new command
prompt/terminal and run the following:

mongo

This will take us to the `mongo` shell, using which we can interface with the MongoDB. The following are a few handy commands:

Description	Command
Show all databases	`show dbs`
Use a specific database	`use local`
Create a database	`use testdb`
Check database in use	`db`
Create a collection	`db.createCollection("user");`
Show all collections in a DB	`show collections`
(Create) insert a document in a collection	`db.user.insert({"name":"arvind"});`
(Read) query a collection	`db.user.find({});`
(Update) modify a document in collection	`db.user.update({"name": "arvind"}, {"name" : "arvind2"}, {"upsert":true});`
(Delete) Remove a document	`db.user.remove({"name": "arvind2"});`

Using the previous commands, you can get acquainted with the Mongo shell. In our API engine, we are going to use Mongoose ODM (http://mongoosejs.com/) to manage from the Node.js/Express--API engine.

Using mLab

If you don't want to go through the hassle of setting up the DB locally, you can use a MongoDB as a service such as mLab (https://mlab.com/) for this. In this book, I am going to follow this approach. Instead of having a local database, I will be using an instance of mLab.

To setup an mLab MongoDB instance, first navigate to https://mlab.com/login/ and login. If you do not have an account, you can create one by navigating to https://mlab.com/signup/.

mLab has a free tier, which we are going to leverage to build our reference architecture. The free tire is perfect for development and prototyping projects like ours. Once we are done with the actual development and we are ready for a production grade application, we can look at some more reliable plans. You can get an idea of pricing at `https://mlab.com/plans/pricing/.`

Once you are logged in, click on the **Create New** button to create a new DB. Now, select **amazon web services** under **Cloud Provider** and then select the **Plan Type** as **FREE**, as shown in the following screenshot:

And finally, name the database as `iotfwjs` and click on **CREATE**. And in a few seconds, a new MongoDB instance should be created for us.

Once the database has been created, open the `iotfwjs` DB. We should see a couple of warnings: one stating that this **sandbox** database should not be used for production, which we are aware of, and the second one that there is no database user present.

So, let's go ahead and create one. Click on the **Users** tab and click on the **Add database user** button and fill in the form with the username as `admin` and password as `admin123` as follows:

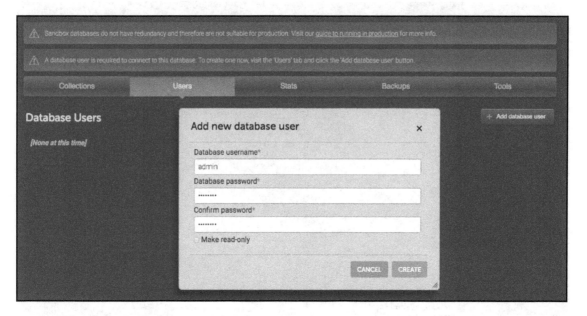

You can choose your own username and password and update it accordingly in the remaining part of the book.

Now to test the connection to our database, use the section at the top of the page to connect using the `mongo` shell. In my case, it is as follows:

Open a new command prompt and run the following (after updating the mLab URL and credentials accordingly):

```
mongo ds241055.mlab.com:41055/iotfwjs -u admin -p admin123
```

We should be able to log in to the shell and we can run queries from here as follows:

```
[→  ~ mongo ds241055.mlab.com:41055/iotfwjs -u admin -p admin123
MongoDB shell version v3.4.2
connecting to: mongodb://ds241055.mlab.com:41055/iotfwjs
MongoDB server version: 3.4.9
[rs-ds241055:PRIMARY> db
iotfwjs
[rs-ds241055:PRIMARY> db.stats();
{
        "db" : "iotfwjs",
        "collections" : 0,
        "views" : 0,
        "objects" : 0,
        "avgObjSize" : 0,
        "dataSize" : 0,
        "storageSize" : 0,
        "numExtents" : 0,
        "indexes" : 0,
        "indexSize" : 0,
        "fileSize" : 0,
        "ok" : 1
}
rs-ds241055:PRIMARY> █
```

This completes our setup of MongoDB.

MQTTS broker - Mosca

In this section, we are going to put together the MQTTS broker. We are going to use Mosca (http://www.mosca.io/) as a standalone service (https://github.com/mcollina/mosca/wiki/Mosca-as-a-standalone-service).

Create a new folder named chapter2. Inside the chapter2 folder, create a new folder named broker and open a new command prompt/terminal inside the folder. Then run the following:

```
npm install mosca pino -g
```

This will install Mosca and Pino globally. Pino (`https://github.com/pinojs/pino`) is a Node.js logger, which logs all the messages to the console thrown by Mosca.

Now, the default version of Mosca implements MQTT. But we want to secure our communication between the smart device and cloud to avoid man-in-the-middle attacks.

So, for us to set up MQTTS, we would need an SSL key and SSL certificate. To create the SSL key and certificate locally, we will use `openssl`.

To check whether `openssl` is present on your machine, run `openssl version -a` and you should see the information about your local installation of `openssl`.

If you don't have `openssl`, you can download the same from `https://www.openssl.org/source/`.

Now, inside the `broker` folder, create another folder named `certs` and `cd` into that folder. Run the following to generate the required key and certificate file:

```
openssl req -newkey rsa:2048 -nodes -keyout key.pem -x509 -days 365 -out
certificate.pem
```

This will prompt a few questions and you can fill in the same along the following lines:

```
[→  certs openssl req -newkey rsa:2048 -nodes -keyout key.pem -x509 -days 365 -out certificate.pem
Generating a 2048 bit RSA private key
........+++
.....................+++
writing new private key to 'key.pem'
-----
You are about to be asked to enter information that will be incorporated
into your certificate request.
What you are about to enter is what is called a Distinguished Name or a DN.
There are quite a few fields but you can leave some blank
For some fields there will be a default value,
If you enter '.', the field will be left blank.
-----
Country Name (2 letter code) [AU]:IN
State or Province Name (full name) [Some-State]:TG
Locality Name (eg, city) []:HYD
Organization Name (eg, company) [Internet Widgits Pty Ltd]:UBICONN
Organizational Unit Name (eg, section) []:THE IOT SUITCASE
Common Name (e.g. server FQDN or YOUR name) []:TIS
Email Address []:arvind.ravulavaru@gmail.com
```

This will create two new files inside the `certs` folder named `key.pem` and `certificate.pem`. We will be using these in our Mosca setup.

Next, at the root of the `broker` folder, create a new file named `index.js` and update it as follows:

```
let SSL_KEY = __dirname + '/certs/key.pem';
let SSL_CERT = __dirname + '/certs/certificate.pem';
let MONGOURL = 'mongodb://admin:admin123@ds241055.mlab.com:41055/iotfwjs';

module.exports = {
    id: 'broker',
    stats: false,
    port: 8443,
    logger: {
        name: 'iotfwjs',
        level: 'debug'
    },
    secure: {
        keyPath: SSL_KEY,
        certPath: SSL_CERT,
    },
    backend: {
        type: 'mongodb',
        url: MONGOURL
    },
    persistence: {
        factory: 'mongo',
        url: MONGOURL
    }
};
```

The previous code is the configuration with which we are going to launch Mosca. The config here loads the SSL certificates and keys and sets Mongo as our persistence layer.

Save `index.js` and head back to the terminal/prompt and `cd` into the location where we have the `index.js` file. Next, run the following:

```
mosca -c index.js -v | pino
```

And we should see the following:

```
[→ broker mosca -c index.js -v | pino
        +++.+++:    ,+++      +++;    '+++      +++.
      ++.+++.++    ++.++  ++,'+   `+',++  ++,++
      +`  +,  +: .+  .+  +;  +;  '+  '+  +`  +`
      +`  +.  +: ,+  `+  ++  +;  '+  ;+  +   +.
      +`  +.  +: ,+  `+  +'      '+      +   +.
      +`  +.  +: ,+  `+  :+.     '+      +++++.
      +`  +.  +: ,+  `+    ++    '+      +++++.
      +`  +.  +: ,+  `+    ++  '+  +   +.
      +`  +.  +: ,+  `+  +:  +:  '+  ;+  +   +.
      +`  +.  +: .+  .+  +;  +;  '+  '+  +   +.
      +`  +.  +: ++;++  ++'++    ++'+'  +   +.
      +`  +.  +:  +++    +++.  ,++'    +   +.
[2017-10-31T11:02:21.546Z] INFO (iotfwjs/12441 on Arvinds-MacBook-Pro.local): server started
    mqtts: 8883
```

As you can see from the previous, we are connected to the `iotfwjs` database and the broker is going to listen to port `8883` for connections.

This wraps up our setup of the MQTTS broker using Mosca.

In the next step, we will implement the API engine and at that point, we are going to test the integration of the MQTTS broker with the API engine.

API engine - Node.js and Express

In this section, we are going to build the API engine. This engine interfaces with our apps and cascades the information from and to the smart device, connecting as an MQTT client with the broker.

To get started, we are going to clone a repository that we have created using a Yeoman (`http://yeoman.io/`) generator named `generator-node-express-mongo` (`https://www.npmjs.com/package/generator-node-express-mongo`). We have taken the code scaffolded by `generator-node-express-mongo` and modified it a bit for our needs.

Somewhere on your machine, download the complete code base of this book using the following command:

```
git clone
https://github.com/PacktPublishing/Practical-Internet-of-Things-with-JavaSc
ript.git
```

Or, you can download the zip file from
`https://github.com/PacktPublishing/Practical-Internet-of-Things-with-JavaScript`
as well.

Once the repository has been downloaded, `cd` into the `base` folder and make a copy of
`api-engine-base` folder into `chapter2` folder.

This will download the `api-engine` boilerplate code. Once the `repo` is cloned, `cd` into the
folder and run the following:

```
npm install
```

This will install the needed dependencies.

If we open the `cloned` folder, we should see the following:

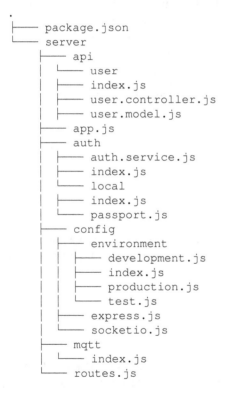

```
.
├── package.json
└── server
    ├── api
    │   └── user
    │       ├── index.js
    │       ├── user.controller.js
    │       ├── user.model.js
    ├── app.js
    ├── auth
    │   ├── auth.service.js
    │   ├── index.js
    │   └── local
    │   ├── index.js
    │   └── passport.js
    ├── config
    │   ├── environment
    │   │   ├── development.js
    │   │   ├── index.js
    │   │   ├── production.js
    │   │   └── test.js
    │   ├── express.js
    │   └── socketio.js
    ├── mqtt
    │   └── index.js
    └── routes.js
```

This folder has all the bare bones needed for us to get started with our API engine.

As you can see from the previous structure, we have a `package.json` at the root of the folder. This file consists of all the dependencies needed. We have also defined our startup script here.

All our application files are present inside the `server` folder. Everything starts at `api-engine/server/app.js`. We initialize `mongoose`, `express`, `socketio`, `config`, `routes`, and `mqtt`. And finally, we start our server and listen to port `9000` on `localhost` with the help of `server.listen()`.

`api-engine/server/config/express.js` has the required setup to initialize the Express middleware. `api-engine/server/config/socketio.js` consists of the logic needed to manage web sockets.

We will be using `api-engine/server/config/environment` to configure the environment variables. For most of the book, we are going to work with the development environment. If we open `api-engine/server/config/environment/development.js`, we should see the configuration for `mongo` and `mqtt`. Update them as follows:

```
// MongoDB connection options
    mongo: {
        uri: 'mongodb://admin:admin123@ds241055.mlab.com:41055/iotfwjs'
    },

    mqtt: {
        host: process.env.EMQTT_HOST || '127.0.0.1',
        clientId: 'API_Server_Dev',
        port: 8883
    }
};
```

 Update the mongo URL as per your setup (mLab or local). Since we are going to connect to the Mosca broker running on our local machine, we are using `127.0.0.1` as the host.

Authorization

Next, we are going to look at out-of-the-box auth. We will be using **JSON Web Tokens (JWTs)** to authenticate the clients that are going to communicate with our API engine. We will be using Passport (`http://passportjs.org/`) for authentication.

Open `api-engine/server/auth/index.js` and we should see the Passport setup using `require('./local/passport').setup(User, config);` and we are creating a new route for authentication.

The routes are configured in `api-engine/server/routes.js`. If we open `api-engine/server/routes.js`, we should see `app.use('/auth', require('./auth'));`. This will create a new endpoint named `/auth` and inside the `api-engine/server/auth/index.js`, we have added `router.use('/local', require('./local'));` now, if we wanted to access the POST method inside `api-engine/server/auth/local/index.js`, we would make a HTTP POST request to `/auth/local`.

In the `api-engine`, we are using the passport local authentication strategy (`https://github.com/jaredhanson/passport-local`) to authenticate the user using MongoDB for persistence.

To create a new user, we are going to use the user API. If we open `api-engine/server/routes.js`, we should see a route defined to access the users collection `app.use('/api/v1/users', require('./api/user'));`. We have prefixed with `/api/v1/users` so we can version our API layer later on.

If we open `api-engine/server/api/user/index.js`, we should the see the following six routes defined:

- `router.get('/', auth.hasRole('admin'), controller.index);`
- `router.delete('/:id', auth.hasRole('admin'), controller.destroy);`
- `router.get('/me', auth.isAuthenticated(), controller.me);`
- `router.put('/:id/password', auth.isAuthenticated(), controller.changePassword);`
- `router.get('/:id', auth.isAuthenticated(), controller.show);`
- `router.post('/', controller.create);`

The first route is for fetching all the users in the database and, using the `auth.hasRole` middleware defined in `api-engine/server/auth/auth.service.js`, we will be checking whether the user is authenticated and has the admin role.

The next route is to delete a user with an ID; after that, we have a route to get a user's information based on the token. We have a `PUT` route to update the user's information; one `GET` route to get a user's information based on the user ID; and finally, a `POST` route to create a user. Do note that the `POST` route doesn't have any authentication or authorization middleware, as the user accessing this endpoint will be using our app for the first time (or is trying to register with us).

Using the `POST` route, we will be creating a new user; this is how we register a user: `api-engine/server/api/user/user.model.js` consists of the Mongoose schema for the user and `api-engine/server/api/user/user.controller.js` consists of the logic for the routes we have defined.

MQTT client

Finally, we are going to look at the MQTT client integration with our `api-engine`. If we open `api-engine/server/mqtt/index.js`, we should see the default setup of the MQTTS client.

We are using the following configuration to connect to the Mosca broker over MQTTS:

```
var client = mqtt.connect({
    port: config.mqtt.port,
    protocol: 'mqtts',
    host: config.mqtt.host,
    clientId: config.mqtt.clientId,
    reconnectPeriod: 1000,
    username: config.mqtt.clientId,
    password: config.mqtt.clientId,
    keepalive: 300,
    rejectUnauthorized: false
});
```

And we are subscribing to two events: one when the connection is established and the other when we receive a message. On the `connect` event, we subscribe to a topic named `greet` and we are publishing a simple message to that topic in the next line. And on the `message` event, we are listening for any messages from the broker and we are printing the topic and the message.

With this, we are aware of most of the pieces of code needed to work with `api-engine`. To start the `api-engine`, `cd` into the `chapter2/api-engine` folder and run the following:

```
npm start
```

This will start a new Express server application on port `9000`.

API engine testing

To quickly check out the API that we have created, we will be using a Chrome extension named Postman. You can set up the Chrome extension from here: `https://chrome.google.com/webstore/detail/postman/fhbjgbiflinjbdggehcddcbncdddo mop?hl=en`.

Once Postman is set up, we will be testing two API calls to validate the register and login methods.

Open Postman and enter the requested URL as `http://localhost:9000/api/v1/users`. Next, select the method type as `POST`. Once that is done, we will set the headers. Add a new header with key as `content-type` and value as `application/json`.

Now we will construct the request body/payload. Click on the **Body** tab, next to **Headers**, and select **Raw** request. And update it with the following:

```
{
    "email" : "arvind@myapp.com",
    "password" : "123456",
    "name" : "Arvind"
}
```

You can update the data as applicable. And then click on **Send**. This makes a request to the API engine, which will in turn save the data to the database and respond with the new user object, along with the auth token.

Our output should be as follows:

Now, if we hit the **Send** button again with the same data, we should see a validation error something the same as the following:

Now, to validate the newly registered user, we will fire a request to `http://localhost:9000/auth/local` with only the email and password. And we should see something the same as the following:

This validates the API we have created.

With this, we complete the walk-through of the API engine. In the next section, we are going to integrate the `api-engine` with the broker and test the connectivity between them.

Communication between broker and API engine

Now that we are done with the two pieces of software on the cloud, we will be interfacing them. In `api-engine/server/config/environment/development.js`, we have defined the broker IP and port that the `api-engine` needs to connect to.

Later on, if we deploy these two pieces on different machines, this is the place where we update the IP and port so the `api-engine` refers to the broker.

Now, to test the communication, `cd` into `chapter2/broker` folder and run the following:

```
mosca -c index.js -v | pino
```

And we should see the following:

```
[→  broker mosca -c index.js -v | pino
        +++.+++:    ,+++     +++;    '+++     +++.
        ++.+++.++   ++.++    ++,'+   `+',++   ++,++
      +`  +,  +: .+   .+   +;  +; '+  '+  +`  +`
      +`  +.  +: ,+   `+   ++  +; '+  ;+  +   +.
      +`  +.  +: ,+   `+   +'      '+      +   +.
      +`  +.  +: ,+   `+   :+.     '+      +++++.
      +`  +.  +: ,+   `+    ++     '+      +++++.
      +`  +.  +: ,+   `+     ++    '+      +   +.
      +`  +.  +: ,+   `+   +:  +: '+  ;+  +   +.
      +`  +.  +: .+   .+   +;  +; '+  '+  +   +.
      +`  +.  +: ++;++   ++'++    ++'+'  +   +.
      +`  +.  +:  +++     +++.   ,++'   +   +.
[2017-10-31T11:46:11.441Z] INFO (iotfwjs/17167 on Arvinds-MacBook-Pro.local): server started
    mqtts: 8883
```

Next, open a new command prompt/terminal, `cd` into `chapter2/api-engine` folder, and run the following:

```
npm start
```

And we should see the following:

```
[nodemon] 1.10.0
[nodemon] to restart at any time, enter `rs`
[nodemon] watching: *.*
[nodemon] starting `node server/app.js`
Express server listening on 9000, in development mode
Connected to Mosca at 127.0.0.1 on port 8883
topic >>> greet
message >>> Hello IoTFWjs
```

The API engine connected to the mLab MongoDB instance, post that it started a new Express server and finally, it connected to the Mosca broker and the posted a message to the greet topic.

Now, if we look at the Mosca terminal, we should see the following:

```
[→  broker mosca -c index.js -v | pino
        +++.+++:      ,+++      +++;    '+++      +++.
       ++.+++.++    ++.++   ++,'+   `+',++   ++,++
       +`   +,   +: .+   .+  +;   +;  '+   '+   +`   +`
       +`   +.   +: ,+   `+  ++   +;  '+   ;+   +    +.
       +`   +.   +: ,+   `+  +'      '+         +    +.
       +`   +.   +: ,+   `+  :+.     '+        +++++.
       +`   +.   +: ,+   `+    ++    '+        +++++.
       +`   +.   +: ,+   `+    ++    '+         +    +.
       +`   +.   +: ,+   `+  +:   +:  '+   ;+   +    +.
       +`   +.   +: .+   .+  +;   +;  '+   '+   +    +.
       +`   +.   +: ++;++   ++'++   ++'+'   +    +.
       +`   +.   +:   +++    +++.   ,++'   +    +.
[2017-10-31T11:46:11.441Z] INFO (iotfwjs/17167 on Arvinds-MacBook-Pro.local): server started
    mqtts: 8883
[2017-10-31T11:46:58.472Z] INFO (iotfwjs/17167 on Arvinds-MacBook-Pro.local): client connected
    client: "API_Server_Dev"
[2017-10-31T11:46:58.492Z] INFO (iotfwjs/17167 on Arvinds-MacBook-Pro.local): subscribed to topic
    topic: "greet"
    qos: 0
    client: "API_Server_Dev"
```

The broker logged the activity that has happened so far. A client connected with username `API_Server_Dev` and subscribed to a topic named greet with **Quality of Service (QoS)** as 0.

With this, our integration between the broker and API engine is complete.

Next, we are going to move towards the Raspberry Pi 3 and start working on an MQTTS client.

 If you are new to MQTT protocol, you can refer to *MQTT Essentials: Part 1 - Introducing MQTT* (http://www.hivemq.com/blog/mqtt-essentials-part-1-introducing-mqtt) and the subsequent parts. To know more about QoS, refer to *MQTT Essentials Part 6: Quality of Service 0, 1 & 2* (https://www.hivemq.com/blog/mqtt-essentials-part-6-mqtt-quality-of-service-levels).

Raspberry Pi software

In this section, we are going to build the required software to make the Raspberry Pi a client to our Mosca broker via the Wi-Fi router.

We have already seen in the data flow diagram how the Raspberry Pi stands between the sensor and the Mosca broker. Now we are going to set up the required code and software.

Setting up Raspberry Pi

In this section, we will look at installing the required software on the Raspberry Pi.

A Raspberry Pi, installed with Raspbian OS
(`https://www.raspberrypi.org/downloads/raspbian/`), is a prerequisite. The Wi-Fi should have already been set up and connected before we continue.

If you are new to setting up a Raspberry Pi 3, refer to the *Beginner's Guide to Installing Node.js on a Raspberry Pi*
(`http://thisdavej.com/beginners-guide-to-installing-node-js-on-a -raspberry-pi/`). We will, however, cover the Node.js part, you can refer until you bring up the Pi and configure the Wi-Fi.

Once the OS is installed, boot up the Raspberry Pi and log in to it. At this point in time, it will be connected to the internet over your own access point and you should be able to browse the internet without issues.

I am accessing my Raspberry Pi 3 from my Apple MacBook Pro using VNC Viewer. This way, I am not always connected to the Raspberry Pi 3.

We will start off by downloading Node.js. Open a new terminal and run the following commands:

```
$ sudo apt update
$ sudo apt full-upgrade
```

This will upgrade all the packages which need upgrades. Next, we will install the latest version of Node.js. At the time of writing, Node 7.x is the latest:

```
$ curl -sL https://deb.nodesource.com/setup_7.x | sudo -E bash -
$ sudo apt install nodejs
```

This will take a moment to install and once your installation is done, you should be able to run the following commands to see the version of Node.js and npm:

```
node -v
npm -v
```

With this, we are done with setting up the required software for running our MQTTS client on the Raspberry Pi 3.

Raspberry Pi MQTTS client

Now we are going to work with the MQTTS client of Node.js.

On the desktop of the Raspberry Pi 3, create a folder named pi-client. Open a terminal and cd into the pi-client folder.

The first thing we are going to do is create a package.json file. From inside the pi-client folder, run the following:

```
$ npm init
```

Then answer the question as applicable. Once you are done with that, next we will install MQTT.js (https://www.npmjs.com/package/mqtt) on the Raspberry Pi 3. Run the following:

```
$ npm install mqtt -save
```

Once this installation is also done, the final package.json will look the same as this:

```
{
    "name": "pi-client",
    "version": "0.1.0",
    "description": "",
    "main": "index.js",
    "scripts": {
        "start": "node index.js"
    },
    "keywords": ["pi", "mqtts"],
    "author": "Arvind Ravulavaru",
    "private": true,
    "license": "ISC",
    "dependencies": {
        "mqtt": "^2.7.1"
    }
}
```

Do note that we have added a start script to launch our `index.js` file. We will be creating the `index.js` file in a moment.

Next, at the root of the `pi-client` folder, create a file named `config.js`. Update `config.js` as follows:

```
module.exports = {
    mqtt: {
        host: '10.2.192.141',
        clientId: 'rPI_3',
        port: 8883
    }
};
```

Do notice the host property. This is set to the IP address of my MacBook and my MacBook is where I am going to run the Mosca broker API engine. Make sure all three (Mosca broker, API engine, and Raspberry Pi 3) of them are on the same Wi-Fi network.

Next, we will write the required MQTT client code. Create a file named `index.js` at the root of the `pi-client` folder and update it as follows:

```
var config = require('./config.js');
var mqtt = require('mqtt')
var client = mqtt.connect({
    port: config.mqtt.port,
    protocol: 'mqtts',
    host: config.mqtt.host,
    clientId: config.mqtt.clientId,
    reconnectPeriod: 1000,
    username: config.mqtt.clientId,
    password: config.mqtt.clientId,
    keepalive: 300,
    rejectUnauthorized: false
});
client.on('connect', function() {
    client.subscribe('greet')
    client.publish('greet', 'Hello, IoTjs!')
});

client.on('message', function(topic, message) {
    // message is Buffer
    console.log('Topic >> ', topic);
    console.log('Message >> ', message.toString())
});
```

This is the same test code we have written on the API engine to test the connectivity. Save all the files and move towards your Mosca broker.

Communication between the broker and the Raspberry Pi

In this section, we are going to communicate between the broker and the Raspberry Pi over MQTTS.

Navigate to the broker folder and run the following:

```
mosca -c index.js -v | pino
```

Next, head over to the Raspberry Pi, cd into the pi-client folder, and run the following:

```
$ npm start
```

And we should see the following message on the Raspberry Pi:

And when we look at the console of Mosca, we should see the following:

```
[→  broker mosca -c index.js -v | pino
        +++.+++:    ,+++    +++;   '+++    +++.
       ++.+++.++   ++.++  ++,'+  `+',++  ++,++
      +`  +,  +: .+  .+  +;  +; '+  '+  +`  +`
      +`  +.  +: ,+  `+  ++  +; '+  ;+  +   +.
      +`  +.  +: ,+  `+  +'     '+      +   +.
      +`  +.  +: ,+  `+  :+.    '+      +++++.
      +`  +.  +: ,+  `+  ++     '+      +++++.
      +`  +.  +: ,+  `+    ++   '+      +   +.
      +`  +.  +: ,+  `+  +:  +: '+  ;+  +   +.
      +`  +.  +: .+  .+  +;  +; '+  '+  +   +.
      +`  +.  +: ++;++  ++'++  ++'+'  +   +.
      +`  +.  +:  +++    +++.   ,++'   +   +.
[2017-05-05T13:36:21.497Z] INFO (iotjs/86004 on Arvinds-MacBook-Pro.local): server started
    mqtts: 8883
[2017-05-05T13:37:29.805Z] INFO (iotjs/86004 on Arvinds-MacBook-Pro.local): client connected
    client: "rPI_3"
[2017-05-05T13:37:29.851Z] INFO (iotjs/86004 on Arvinds-MacBook-Pro.local): subscribed to topic
    topic: "greet"
    qos: 0
    client: "rPI_3"
```

This wraps up our connectivity test between the Raspberry Pi 3 and the Mosca broker.

Troubleshooting

If you are not able to see the previous messages, check the following:

- Check whether the Raspberry Pi and the machine running the broker are on the same Wi-Fi network
- Cross-check the IP address of the machine running the broker

Communication between the Raspberry Pi, the broker and the API engine

Now we are going to integrate the Raspberry Pi, the broker, and the API engine and pass the data from the Pi to the API engine.

The way we are going to achieve this is that we are going create a topic named `api-engine` and another topic named `rpi`.

To send data from the Raspberry Pi to the API engine, we will be using the `api-engine` topic and when we need to send data from the API engine to the Raspberry Pi, we will use the `rpi` topic.

In this example, we are going to get the MAC address of the Raspberry Pi and send that to the API engine. The API engine will acknowledge the same by sending the same MAC address back to the Raspberry Pi. The communication between the API engine and Raspberry Pi will happen over the two topics mentioned previously.

So first, we will update the `api-engine/server/mqtt/index.js` as follows:

```
var mqtt = require('mqtt');
var config = require('../config/environment');

var client = mqtt.connect({
    port: config.mqtt.port,
    protocol: 'mqtts',
    host: config.mqtt.host,
    clientId: config.mqtt.clientId,
    reconnectPeriod: 1000,
    username: config.mqtt.clientId,
    password: config.mqtt.clientId,
    keepalive: 300,
    rejectUnauthorized: false
});

client.on('connect', function() {
    client.subscribe('api-engine');
});

client.on('message', function(topic, message) {
    // message is Buffer
    // console.log('Topic >> ', topic);
    // console.log('Message >> ', message.toString());
    if (topic === 'api-engine') {
        var macAddress = message.toString();
        console.log('Mac Address >> ', macAddress);
        client.publish('rpi', 'Got Mac Address: ' + macAddress);
    } else {
        console.log('Unknown topic', topic);
    }
});
```

Here, once the MQTT connection is established, we are subscribing to the `api-engine` topic. When we receive any data from the `api-engine` topic, we will send back the same to the `rpi` topic.

From inside the `broker` folder, run the following:

```
mosca -c index.js -v | pino
```

Next, from inside the `api-engine` folder, run the following:

```
npm start
```

Next, head back to the Raspberry Pi. We are going to install the `getmac` module (`https://www.npmjs.com/package/getmac`) that will help us to get the MAC address of a device.

From inside the `pi-client` folder, run the following:

```
$ npm install getmac --save
```

Once this is done, update `/home/pi/Desktop/pi-client/index.js` as follows:

```
var config = require('./config.js');
var mqtt = require('mqtt');
var GetMac = require('getmac');

var client = mqtt.connect({
    port: config.mqtt.port,
    protocol: 'mqtts',
    host: config.mqtt.host,
    clientId: config.mqtt.clientId,
    reconnectPeriod: 1000,
    username: config.mqtt.clientId,
    password: config.mqtt.clientId,
    keepalive: 300,
    rejectUnauthorized: false
});

client.on('connect', function() {
    client.subscribe('rpi');
    GetMac.getMac(function(err, macAddress) {
        if (err) throw err;
        client.publish('api-engine', macAddress);
    });
});

client.on('message', function(topic, message) {
```

```
// message is Buffer
// console.log('Topic >> ', topic);
// console.log('Message >> ', message.toString());
if (topic === 'rpi') {
    console.log('API Engine Response >> ', message.toString());
} else {
    console.log('Unknown topic', topic);
}
});
```

In the previous code, we have waited for the connection to establish between the Raspberry Pi and the broker. Once that is done, we have subscribed to the `rpi` topic. Next, we fetched the MAC address of the Raspberry Pi using `GetMac.getMac()` and published the same to the `api-engine` topic.

In the `message` event callback, we are listening for the `rpi` topic. If we receive any data from the server, it will be printed here.

Save the file and from inside the `pi-client` folder, run the following:

```
$ npm start
```

Now, if we look at the broker terminal/prompt, we should see the following:

```
|→  broker mosca -c index.js -v | pino
      +++.+++:     ,+++       +++;     '+++      +++.
      ++.+++.++     ++.++    ++,'+    `+',++    ++,++
     +`   +,   +: .+   .+   +;  +;  '+  '+   +`   +`
     +`   +.   +: ,+   `+   ++  +;  '+  ;+   +    +.
     +`   +.   +: ,+   `+   +'       '+        +     +.
     +`   +.   +: ,+   `+   :+.      '+       +++++.
     +`   +.   +: ,+   `+   ++       '+       +++++.
     +`   +.   +: ,+   `+     ++     '+       +    +.
     +`   +.   +: ,+   `+  +:  +:  '+  ;+   +    +.
     +`   +.   +: .+   .+   +;  +;  '+  '+   +    +.
     +`   +.   +: ++;++    ++'++    ++'+'   +    +.
     +`   +.   +:   +++      +++.    ,++'   +    +.
[2017-05-05T14:00:46.253Z] INFO (iotjs/87678 on Arvinds-MacBook-Pro.local): server started
    mqtts: 8883
[2017-05-05T14:00:47.496Z] INFO (iotjs/87678 on Arvinds-MacBook-Pro.local): client connected
    client: "API_Server_Dev"
[2017-05-05T14:00:47.509Z] INFO (iotjs/87678 on Arvinds-MacBook-Pro.local): subscribed to topic
    topic: "api-engine"
    qos: 0
    client: "API_Server_Dev"
[2017-05-05T14:00:47.610Z] INFO (iotjs/87678 on Arvinds-MacBook-Pro.local): client connected
    client: "rPI_3"
[2017-05-05T14:00:47.669Z] INFO (iotjs/87678 on Arvinds-MacBook-Pro.local): subscribed to topic
    topic: "rpi"
    qos: 0
    client: "rPI_3"
```

Both the devices are connected and subscribed to the topic of interest.

Next, if we look at the `api-engine` terminal/prompt, we should see the following:

```
[→  api-engine npm start

> api-engine@0.1.0 start /Users/arvindravulavaru/Arvind/Books/Advanced IoT with JS/code/chapter2/api-engine
> nodemon server/app.js

[nodemon] 1.11.0
[nodemon] to restart at any time, enter `rs`
[nodemon] watching: *.*
[nodemon] starting `node server/app.js`
Express server listening on 9000, in development mode
Mac Address >>  b8:27:eb:f3:2d:4a
```

And finally, the Raspberry Pi terminal should look the same as this:

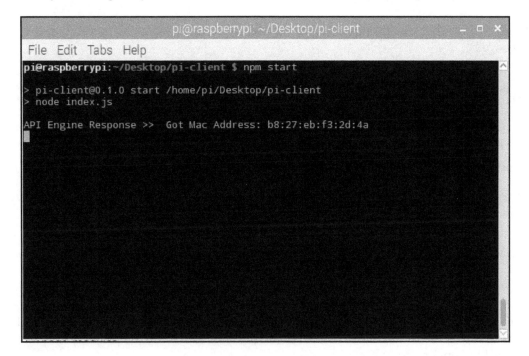

With this, we conclude the integration of the Raspberry Pi with the broker and API engine.

In the next section, we will implement a web application that can send and receive data from the Raspberry Pi through the broker and API engine.

Web app

In this section, we are going to build a web app that interfaces with our API engine. The web app is the primary interface with which we will be interacting with our smart devices.

We are going to build the web app using Angular (4) and Twitter Bootstrap (3). There is no rule that the interface should be built with Angular and Bootstrap; it can be built using jQuery or React.js as well. All we will be doing is interfacing with the APIs of the API engine using JavaScript from the browser. The only reason we are using Angular is to keep the framework consistent across all our apps. Since we will be using the Ionic framework, which also follows the Angular approach, things will be easy for us to manage as well as reuse.

To get started with the web application, we are going to install Angular CLI (`https://github.com/angular/angular-cli`).

On the machine that was running our broker and API engine, we will be setting up the web app as well.

Setting up the app

From inside the `chapter2` folder, open a new command prompt/terminal and run the following:

```
npm install -g @angular/cli
```

This will install the Angular CLI generator. If you run `ng -v` after the installation is done, you should see a version number greater than or equal to 1.0.2.

 If you are facing any issues while setting up and running the IoTFW.js, feel free to drop your comment here:
`https://github.com/PacktPublishing/Practical-Internet-of-Things-with-JavaScript/issues/1`

For the web app, we have already created a base project using Angular CLI and have added the essential pieces to integrate with the API engine. We will clone the project as is and then start working on top of it.

To get started, we need the web app base. If you have not already cloned the book's code repository, you can do so using the following command-line (anywhere on your machine):

```
git clone git@github.com:PacktPublishing/Practical-Internet-of-Things-with-JavaScript.git
```

Or you can download the zip file from
`https://github.com/PacktPublishing/Practical-Internet-of-Things-with-JavaScript`
as well.

Once the repository has been downloaded, `cd` into the `base` folder and make a copy of
`web-app-base` folder into `chapter2` folder.

Once the base has been copied, `cd` into the `web-app` folder, and run the following
command:

```
npm install
```

This will install the needed dependencies.

Project structure

If we open the `cloned` folder, we should see the following:

```
.
├── README.md
├── e2e
│   ├── app.e2e-spec.ts
│   ├── app.po.ts
│   └── tsconfig.e2e.json
├── karma.conf.js
├── package.json
├── protractor.conf.js
├── src
│   ├── app
│   │   ├── add-device
│   │   │   ├── add-device.component.css
│   │   │   ├── add-device.component.html
│   │   │   ├── add-device.component.spec.ts
│   │   │   └── add-device.component.ts
│   │   ├── app.component.css
│   │   ├── app.component.html
│   │   ├── app.component.spec.ts
│   │   ├── app.component.ts
│   │   ├── app.global.ts
│   │   ├── app.module.ts
│   │   ├── device
│   │   │   ├── device.component.css
│   │   │   ├── device.component.html
│   │   │   ├── device.component.spec.ts
│   │   │   └── device.component.ts
│   │   ├── device-template
```

```
│   │   │   ├──── device-template.component.css
│   │   │   ├──── device-template.component.html
│   │   │   ├──── device-template.component.spec.ts
│   │   │   └──── device-template.component.ts
│   │   ├──── guard
│   │   │   ├──── auth.guard.spec.ts
│   │   │   └──── auth.guard.ts
│   │   ├──── home
│   │   │   ├──── home.component.css
│   │   │   ├──── home.component.html
│   │   │   ├──── home.component.spec.ts
│   │   │   └──── home.component.ts
│   │   ├──── login
│   │   │   ├──── login.component.css
│   │   │   ├──── login.component.html
│   │   │   ├──── login.component.spec.ts
│   │   │   └──── login.component.ts
│   │   ├──── nav-bar
│   │   │   ├──── nav-bar.component.css
│   │   │   ├──── nav-bar.component.html
│   │   │   ├──── nav-bar.component.spec.ts
│   │   │   └──── nav-bar.component.ts
│   │   ├──── register
│   │   │   ├──── register.component.css
│   │   │   ├──── register.component.html
│   │   │   ├──── register.component.spec.ts
│   │   │   └──── register.component.ts
│   │   └──── services
│   │   ├──── auth.service.spec.ts
│   │   ├──── auth.service.ts
│   │   ├──── data.service.spec.ts
│   │   ├──── data.service.ts
│   │   ├──── devices.service.spec.ts
│   │   ├──── devices.service.ts
│   │   ├──── http-interceptor.service.spec.ts
│   │   ├──── http-interceptor.service.ts
│   │   ├──── loader.service.spec.ts
│   │   ├──── loader.service.ts
│   │   ├──── socket.service.spec.ts
│   │   └──── socket.service.ts
│   ├──── assets
│   ├──── environments
│   │   ├──── environment.prod.ts
│   │   └──── environment.ts
│   ├──── favicon.ico
│   ├──── index.html
│   ├──── main.ts
│   ├──── polyfills.ts
```

```
|    ├──── styles.css
|    ├──── test.ts
|    ├──── tsconfig.app.json
|    ├──── tsconfig.spec.json
|    └──── typings.d.ts
├──── tsconfig.json
└──── tslint.json
```

Now, for the walk-through of the project structure and code setup.

At a high level, we have an `src` folder, where we will have all the source code and unit test code, and an `e2e` folder, which consists of the end-to-end test.

We will be spending most of the time inside the `src/app` folder. Before we go into this folder, open `web-app/src/main.ts` and this is where everything begins. Next, we have added the Twitter Bootstrap Cosmos theme (`https://bootswatch.com/cosmo/`) here and defined a few layout styles.

Now, the `app/src` folder: here, we have defined the root component, the root module, and the required components and services.

App module

Open `web-app/src/app/app.module.ts`. This file consists of the `@NgModule` declaration, which defines all the components and services that we are going to use.

We have created the following components:

- `AppComponent`: Application root component that holds the router outlet
- `NavBarComponent`: This is the navigation bar component that appears on the all the pages. This component automatically detects the authentication state and shows the menu bar accordingly
- `LoginComponent`: This deals with the login feature
- `RegisterComponent`: To work with registration with the API engine
- `HomeComponent`: This component displays all the devices attached to the current logged-in user
- `DeviceComponent`: This component displays information about one device
- `AddDeviceComponent`: This component lets us add a new component to our device list
- `DeviceTemplateComponent`: A common template that is used to represent a device in our application

Apart from the previous, we have also added the required modules to the imports:

- `RouterModule`: To manage the routing
- `LocalStorageModule`: To manage the user data within the browser, we are going to use `LocalStorgae`
- `SimpleNotificationsModule` : To show the notifications using Angular 2 notifications (`https://github.com/flauc/angular2-notifications`)

And for the services, we have the following:

- `AuthService`: To manage the authentication APIs exposed by the API engine
- `DevicesService`: To manage the device API exposed by the API engine
- `DataService`: To manage the Data API exposed by the API engine
- `SocketService`: To manage web sockets that send data from the API engine in real time
- `AuthGuard`: An Angular Guard that protects routes which need authentication. Read *Protecting Routes using Guards in Angular* (`https://blog.thoughtram.io/angular/2016/07/18/guards-in-angular-2.html`) for more information on Guards
- `LoaderService`: That shows and hides a loader bar when an activity is going on
- `Http`: The HTTP service that we use to make HTTP requests. Here, we have not used the HTTP service as is, but extended the class and added our logic in between to manage the HTTP request experience better using the loader service

Do note that at this point, the API engine does not have APIs for devices and data, and sockets are not set up for the data. We will be implementing in the API engine, once we are done with the web app completely.

In this web application, we are going to have the following routes:

- `login`: To let the user log in to the application
- `register`: To register with our application
- `home`: A page that displays all the devices in a user account
- `add-device`: A page to add a new device to the user's device list
- `view-device/:id`: A page to view one device, identified by the id parameter in the URL
- `**`: The default route is set to login
- `''`: If no route matches, we redirect the user to the login page

Web app services

Now that we understand at a high level all that is present in this web app, we will walk through the services and components.

Open `web-app/src/app/services/http-interceptor.service.ts`; in this class, we have extended the `Http` class and implemented the class methods. We have added two methods of our own named `requestInterceptor()` and `responseInterceptor()`, which intercept the request and response respectively.

When the request is about to be sent, we call the `requestInterceptor()` to show a loader, indicating the HTTP activity, and we use the `responseInterceptor()` to hide the loader once the response arrives. This way, the user is clearly aware if there is any background activity going on.

Next is the `LoaderService` class; open `web-app/src/app/services/loader.service.ts` and, as we can see from here, we have added a class property named status of the type `BehaviorSubject<boolean>` (to know more about `Behaviour` subject, refer to `https://github.com/Reactive-Extensions/RxJS/blob/master/doc/api/subjects/behaviorsubject.md`). And we have a method, which will be called by the HTTP service or any other component if they would like to show or hide the loader bar and then set the value as true or false.

The required HTML for the loader service is present in `web-app/src/app/app.component.html` and the required styles are present in `web-app/src/app/app.component.css`.

We are going to use web sockets for streaming data in real time between the web app and the API engine. Open `web-app/src/app/services/socket.service.ts` and we should see the constructor and the `getData()` method. We are using `socket.io-client` (`https://github.com/socketio/socket.io-client`) to manage web sockets in our web app.

In the constructor, we have created a new socket connection to our API engine and passed the auth token as a query parameter. We are going to validate the incoming connections via web sockets as well. And only if the token is valid will we allow the connection, else we close the web socket.

Inside `getData()`, we subscribe to the `data:save` topic for a device. This is how we get notified from the API engine when there is new data available from a device.

Now we will look at the three API services with which we authenticate the user, get the user's devices and get data for a device:

- `AuthService`: Open `web-app/src/app/services/auth.service.ts`. Here, we have defined the `register()`, `login()`, and `logout()`, which takes care of managing the authentication state and we have `isAuthenticated()`, which returns the current state of authentication, as in whether the user is logged in or logged out.
- `DevicesService`: Open `web-app/src/app/services/devices.service.ts`. Here, we have implemented three methods: one to create, one to read, and one to delete. With this, we manage our devices for a user.
- `DataService`: Open `web-app/src/app/services/data.service.ts`, which manages the data for a device. We have only two methods here: one to create a new data record and one to fetch the last 30 records of a device.

Do notice that we are using `web-app/src/app/app.global.ts` to save all our constant global variables.

Now that we are done with the required services, we will walk through the components.

Web app components

We will start with the app component. The app component is the root component, which holds the router outlet, loader service HTML, and notification service HTML. You can find the same here: `web-app/src/app/app.component.html`. In `web-app/src/app/app.component.ts`, we have defined `showLoader` that decides whether the loader should be shown or not. We have also defined notification options, which stores the notification service configurations.

Inside the constructor, we are listening for route change events on the router, so we can show a loading bar on page change. We are also listening to the loader service status variable. If this changes, we show or hide the loader.

The first page that the user lands on is the login page. The login page/component, `web-app/src/app/login/login.component.ts`, has only one method, the takes the user's email and password from `web-app/src/app/login/login.component.html` and authenticates the user.

Using the register button on the home page, the user registers themself. Inside the `RegisterComponent` class, `web-app/src/app/register/register.component.ts`, we have defined `register()`, which takes the user's information and, using the `AuthService`, registers a user.

Once the user has been successfully authenticated, we redirect the user to the `LoginComponent`. In the `HomeComponent`, `web-app/src/app/home/home.component.ts`, we fetch all the devices associated with the user and display them on load. This page also has a button for adding a new device using the `AddDeviceComponent`.

To view one device, we use the `DeviceComponent` to view one device.

As of now, we do not have any APIs available to work with devices and data. We will revisit this page once we finish the API engine update in the next section.

Launching the app

To run the app, open a terminal/prompt inside the `web-app` folder and run the following:

```
ng serve
```

 Make sure the API engine and Mosca are running before you run the previous command.

Once the webpack compilation is successful, navigate to `http://localhost:4200/login` and we should see the login page, this is the first page:

We can use the account we have created while testing the API engine, using Postman, or we can create a new account by clicking on **Register with Web App** as follows:

If the registration is successful, we should be redirected to the home page as follows:

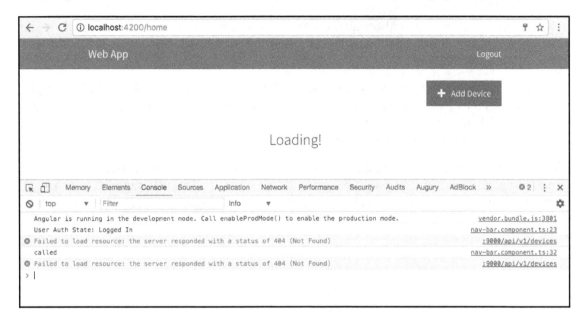

If we open the developer tools, we should see the previous message. The API engine does not have APIs for devices implemented, hence the previous 404s. We will fix that in Chapter 3, *IoTFW.js - II*.

We will also walk through the remaining part of the web app in Chapter 3, *IoTFW.js - II*, once we are done with the API engine update.

Summary

In this chapter, we have gone through the process of setting up a frame to work with internet of Things solutions. We have built most of the framework using only JavaScript as our programming language.

We started by understanding the architecture and data flow from a Raspberry Pi to an end user device such as a web app, desktop app, or mobile app. Then we started working on the broker using Mosca, after setting up the MongoDB. Next, we designed and developed the API engine and completed the basic Raspberry Pi setup.

We have worked on the web app and set up the necessary templates to work with the remaining part of the application. In Chapter 3, *IoTFW.js - II*, we will complete the entire framework and also integrate a DHT11 (temperature and humidity) sensor and an LED to validate the two-way data flow end to end.

3
IoTFW.js - II

In the previous chapter, we have seen the basic setup among Raspberry Pi, broker, API engine, and the web app. In this chapter, we will work on the remaining part of the framework. We will also build a simple example that involves sensing and actuating. We will read temperature and humidity using a temperature and humidity sensor and also turn on/off an LED connected to our Raspberry Pi using web, desktop, or mobile app.

We will cover the following topics in this chapter:

- Updating the API engine
- Integrating the API engine with web app
- Building an end-to-end example using DHT11 and LED
- Building a desktop app
- Building a mobile app

Updating the API engine

Now that we are done with the web app development, we will update the API engine to add the device's API and data service, along with web sockets.

Open `api-engine/server/routes.js`; we will add two routes here. Update `api-engine/server/routes.js`, as follows:

```
'use strict';

var path = require('path');

module.exports = function(app) {
  // Insert routes below
```

```
    app.use('/api/v1/users', require('./api/user'));
    app.use('/api/v1/devices', require('./api/device'));
    app.use('/api/v1/data', require('./api/data'));

    app.use('/auth', require('./auth'));
};
```

Now, we will add the definitions for these routes. Inside the `api-engine/server/api` folder, create a new folder named `device`. Inside the `device` folder, create a new file named `index.js`. Update `api-engine/server/api/device/index.js`, as follows:

```
'use strict';

var express = require('express');
var controller = require('./device.controller');
var config = require('../../config/environment');
var auth = require('../../auth/auth.service');

var router = express.Router();

router.get('/', auth.isAuthenticated(), controller.index);
router.delete('/:id', auth.isAuthenticated(), controller.destroy);
router.put('/:id', auth.isAuthenticated(), controller.update);
router.get('/:id', auth.isAuthenticated(), controller.show);
router.post('/', auth.isAuthenticated(), controller.create);

module.exports = router;
```

Here, we have added five routes, as follows:

- Get all devices
- Delete a device
- Update a device
- Get one device
- Create a device

Next, create another file inside the `api-engine/server/api/device/` folder named `device.model.js`. This file will consist of the mongoose schema for the device collection. Update `api-engine/server/api/device/device.model.js`, as follows:

```
'use strict';

var mongoose = require('mongoose');
var Schema = mongoose.Schema;
```

```
var DeviceSchema = new Schema({
    name: String,
    macAddress: String,
    createdBy: {
        type: String,
        default: 'user'
    },
    createdAt: {
        type: Date
    },
    updatedAt: {
        type: Date
    }
});

DeviceSchema.pre('save', function(next) {
    var now = new Date();
    this.updatedAt = now;
    if (!this.createdAt) {
        this.createdAt = now;
    }
    next();
});

module.exports = mongoose.model('Device', DeviceSchema);
```

Finally, the controller logic. Create a file named `device.controller.js` inside the api-engine/server/api/device folder and update api-engine/server/api/device/device.controller.js, as follows:

```
'use strict';

var Device = require('./device.model');

/**
 * Get list of all devices for a user
 */
exports.index = function(req, res) {
    var currentUser = req.user._id;
    // get only devices related to the current user
    Device.find({
        createdBy: currentUser
    }, function(err, devices) {
        if (err) return res.status(500).send(err);
        res.status(200).json(devices);
    });
};
```

```
/**
 * Add a new device
 */
exports.create = function(req, res, next) {
    var device = req.body;
    // this device is created by the current user
    device.createdBy = req.user._id;
    Device.create(device, function(err, device) {
        if (err) return res.status(500).send(err);
        res.json(device);
    });
};

/**
 * Get a single device
 */
exports.show = function(req, res, next) {
    var deviceId = req.params.id;
    // the current user should have created this device
    Device.findOne({
        _id: deviceId,
        createdBy: req.user._id
    }, function(err, device) {
        if (err) return res.status(500).send(err);
        if (!device) return res.status(404).end();
        res.json(device);
    });
};

/**
 * Update a device
 */
exports.update = function(req, res, next) {
    var device = req.body;
    device.createdBy = req.user._id;

    Device.findOne({
        _id: deviceId,
        createdBy: req.user._id
    }, function(err, device) {
        if (err) return res.status(500).send(err);
        if (!device) return res.status(404).end();

        device.save(function(err, updatedDevice) {
            if (err) return res.status(500).send(err);
            return res.status(200).json(updatedDevice);
        });
    });
```

```
};

/**
 * Delete a device
 */
exports.destroy = function(req, res) {
    Device.findOne({
        _id: req.params.id,
        createdBy: req.user._id
    }, function(err, device) {
        if (err) return res.status(500).send(err);

        device.remove(function(err) {
            if (err) return res.status(500).send(err);
            return res.status(204).end();
        });
    });
};
```

Here, we have defined the logic for the routes.

The device API manages the device for us. To manage the data for each device, we will use this collection.

Now, we will define the data APIs. Create a new folder named data inside the api-engine/server/api folder. Inside the api-engine/server/api/data folder, create a new file named index.js and update api-engine/server/api/data/index.js, as follows:

```
'use strict';

var express = require('express');
var controller = require('./data.controller');
var auth = require('../../auth/auth.service');

var router = express.Router();

router.get('/:deviceId/:limit', auth.isAuthenticated(), controller.index);
router.post('/', auth.isAuthenticated(), controller.create);

module.exports = router;
```

We have defined two routes here: one to view data based on a device ID and another to create data. The view data route returns the data from a device that is limited to the number passed in as part of the request. If you remember, in the web-app/src/app/services/data.service.ts, we have defined the dataLimit class variable as 30. This is the number of records we get, at a given time, from the API.

Next, for the mongoose schema, create a new file named data.model.js inside the api-engine/server/api/data folder and update api-engine/server/api/data/data.model.js, as follows:

```
'use strict';

var mongoose = require('mongoose');
var Schema = mongoose.Schema;

var DataSchema = new Schema({
    macAddress: {
        type: String
    },
    data: {
        type: Schema.Types.Mixed
    },
    createdBy: {
        type: String,
        default: 'raspberrypi3'
    },
    createdAt: {
        type: Date
    },
    updatedAt: {
        type: Date
    }
});

DataSchema.pre('save', function(next) {
    var now = new Date();
    this.updatedAt = now;
    if (!this.createdAt) {
        this.createdAt = now;
    }
    next();
});
```

```
DataSchema.post('save', function(doc) {
    //console.log('Post Save Called', doc);
    require('./data.socket.js').onSave(doc)
});

module.exports = mongoose.model('Data', DataSchema);
```

Now, the controller logic for the data API. Create a file named `data.controller.js` inside `api-engine/server/api/data` and update `api-engine/server/api/data/data.controller.js`, as follows:

```
'use strict';

var Data = require('./data.model');

/**
 * Get Data for a device
 */
exports.index = function(req, res) {
    var macAddress = req.params.deviceId;
    var limit = parseInt(req.params.limit) || 30;
    Data.find({
        macAddress: macAddress
    }).limit(limit).exec(function(err, devices) {
        if (err) return res.status(500).send(err);
        res.status(200).json(devices);
    });
};

/**
 * Create a new data record
 */
exports.create = function(req, res, next) {
    var data = req.body;
    data.createdBy = req.user._id;
    Data.create(data, function(err, _data) {
        if (err) return res.status(500).send(err);
        res.json(_data);
        if(data.topic === 'led'){
            require('../../mqtt/index.js').sendLEDData(data.data.l);// send
led value
        }
    });
};
```

Here, we have defined two methods: one for getting data for a device and one for creating a new data record for a device.

For the data API, we will implement sockets as well, so when a new record comes from the Raspberry Pi, we immediately notify the web app, desktop app, or mobile app so that the data can be displayed in real time.

As we see from the preceding code, if the incoming topic is LED, we will call the sendLEDData(), which in turns publishes the data to the device.

Create a file named data.socket.js inside the api-engine/server/api/data folder and update api-engine/server/api/data/data.socket.js, as follows:

```
/**
 * Broadcast updates to client when the model changes
 */

'use strict';

var data = require('./data.model');
var socket = undefined;

exports.register = function(_socket) {
    socket = _socket;
}

function onSave(doc) {
    // send data to only the intended device
    socket.emit('data:save:' + doc.macAddress, doc);
}


module.exports.onSave = onSave;
```

This will take care of sending a new data record as it successfully gets saved in the database.

Next, we need to add the socket to the socket configuration. Open api-engine/server/config/socketio.js and update it, as follows:

```
'use strict';

var config = require('./environment');

// When the user disconnects.. perform this
function onDisconnect(socket) {}
```

```
// When the user connects.. perform this
function onConnect(socket) {
    // Insert sockets below
    require('../api/data/data.socket').register(socket);
}
module.exports = function(socketio) {
    socketio.use(require('socketio-jwt').authorize({
        secret: config.secrets.session,
        handshake: true
    }));

    socketio.on('connection', function(socket) {
        var socketId = socket.id;
        var clientIp = socket.request.connection.remoteAddress;

        socket.address = socket.handshake.address !== null ?
            socket.handshake.address.address + ':' +
socket.handshake.address.port :
            process.env.DOMAIN;

        socket.connectedAt = new Date();

        // Call onDisconnect.
        socket.on('disconnect', function() {
            onDisconnect(socket);
            // console.info('[%s] DISCONNECTED', socket.address);
        });

        // Call onConnect.
        onConnect(socket);
        console.info('[%s] Connected on %s', socketId, clientIp);
    });
};
```

Note that we are using `socketio-jwt` to validate the socket connection to see if it has JWT. If a valid JWT is not provided, we do not allow the client to connect.

With this, we are done with the required changes to the API engine. Save all the files and launch the API engine by running the following command:

npm start

This will launch the API engine. In the next section, we will test the integration between the web app and API engine and continue our walk through from the previous section.

Integrating web app and API engine

Launch the broker, API engine, and web app. Once all of them are successfully launched, navigate to `http://localhost:4200/`. Log in with the credentials we have created. Once we have successfully logged in, we should see the following screen:

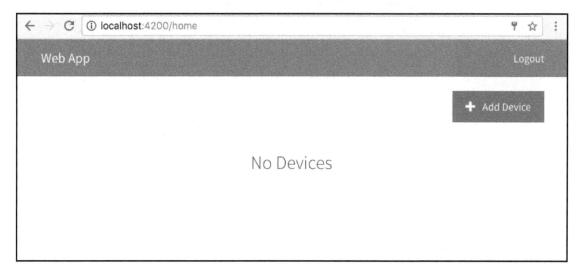

Which is true, as we do not have any devices in our account. Click on **Add Device** and we should see something as follows:

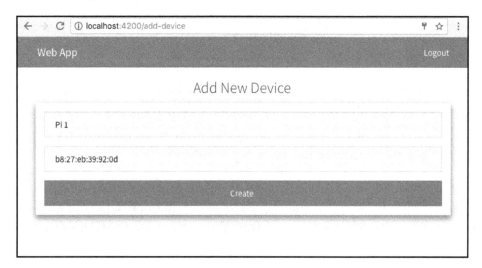

Add a new device by giving it a name. I named my device `Pi 1` and added the mac address. We will use the mac address of the device as a unique way of identifying the device.

Click on **Create** and we should see a new device created, it will redirect us to the home page and display the newly created device, which can be seen in the following screenshot:

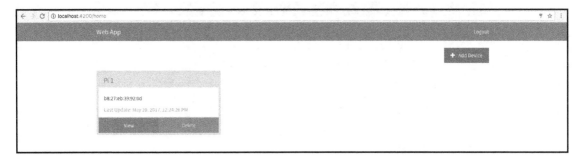

Now, when we click on the **View** button, we should see the following page:

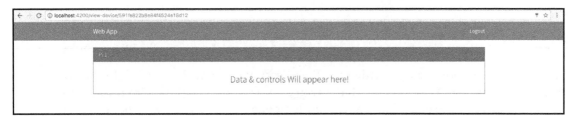

In the examples across this book, we will keep updating this template and keep modifying it as we need to. For now, this is a dummy template represented by `web-app/src/app/device/device.component.html`.

If we open the developer tools and look at the network tab WS section, as shown in the following screenshot, we should be able to see that a web socket request is sent to our server with the JWT token:

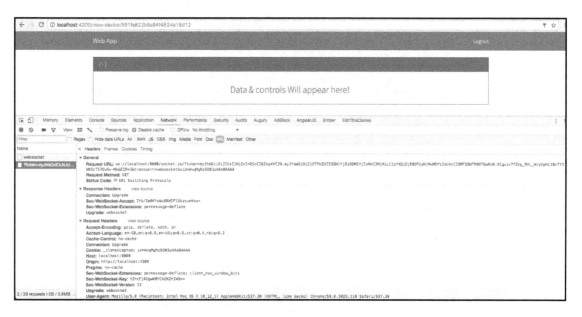

With this, we are done with stitching the Raspberry Pi with the broker, the broker with the API engine, and the API engine with the web app. To complete the entire round trip of data from the device to the web app, we will implement a simple use case in the next section.

Testing an end-to-end flow using DHT11 and LED

Before we start working on the desktop and mobile app, we will implement an end-to-end data flow for the Raspberry Pi to the web app and back.

The example that we will work on implements an actuator and a sensor use case. We will connect an LED to the Raspberry Pi and turn the LED on/off from the web app, and we will also connect a DHT11 temperature sensor to the Raspberry Pi and view its values in real time on the web app.

We will get started with the Raspberry Pi, implement the required logic there; next, work with the API engine, make the required changes, and finally the web app to represent the data.

Setting up and updating the Raspberry Pi

First, we will set up the circuit, as follows:

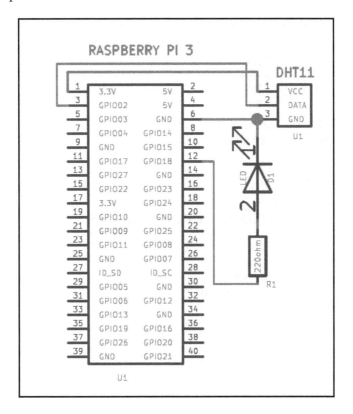

Now, we will make the following connections:

Source pin	Component pin
Raspberry Pi pin 1 - 3.3V	Breadboard + railing
Raspberry Pi pin 6 - Ground	Breadboard - railing
Raspberry Pi pin 3 - GPIO 2	Temperature sensor signal pin
Raspberry Pi pin 12 - GPIO 18	LED anode pin
LED cathode pin	Breadboard - railing
Temperature sensor + pin	Breadboard + railing
Temperature sensor - pin	Breadboard - railing

 We have used a current limiting resistor of 220 ohms between pin 12/GPIO 18 and the anode of a LED pin.

Once this connection has been set up, we will write the required logic. On the Raspberry Pi, open the `pi-client/index.js` file and update it, as follows:

```
var config = require('./config.js');
var mqtt = require('mqtt');
var GetMac = require('getmac');
var rpiDhtSensor = require('rpi-dht-sensor');
var rpio = require('rpio');
var dht11 = new rpiDhtSensor.DHT11(2);
var temp = 0,
    prevTemp = 0;
var humd = 0,
    prevHumd = 0;
var macAddress;
var state = 0;

// Set pin 12 as output pin and to low
rpio.open(12, rpio.OUTPUT, rpio.LOW);

var client = mqtt.connect({
    port: config.mqtt.port,
    protocol: 'mqtts',
    host: config.mqtt.host,
    clientId: config.mqtt.clientId,
    reconnectPeriod: 1000,
```

```
        username: config.mqtt.clientId,
        password: config.mqtt.clientId,
        keepalive: 300,
        rejectUnauthorized: false
});

client.on('connect', function() {
    client.subscribe('rpi');
    client.subscribe('led');
    GetMac.getMac(function(err, mac) {
        if (err) throw err;
        macAddress = mac;
        client.publish('api-engine', mac);
    });
});

client.on('message', function(topic, message) {
    message = message.toString();
    if (topic === 'rpi') {
        console.log('API Engine Response >> ', message);
    } else if (topic === 'led') {
        state = parseInt(message)
        console.log('Turning LED', state ? 'On' : 'Off');
        // If we get a 1 we turn on the led, else off
        rpio.write(12, state ? rpio.HIGH : rpio.LOW);
    } else {
        console.log('Unknown topic', topic);
    }
});

// infinite loop, with 3 seconds delay
setInterval(function() {
    getDHT11Values();
    console.log('Temperature: ' + temp + 'C, ' + 'humidity: ' + humd +
'%');
    // if the temperature and humidity values change
    // then only publish the values
    if (temp !== prevTemp || humd !== prevHumd) {
        var data2Send = {
            data: {
                t: temp,
                h: humd,
                l: state
            },
            macAddress: macAddress
        };
        console.log('Data Published');
        client.publish('dht11', JSON.stringify(data2Send));
```

```
            // reset prev values to current
            // for next loop
            prevTemp = temp;
            prevHumd = humd;
        } // else chill!

    }, 3000); // every three second

    function getDHT11Values() {
        var readout = dht11.read();
        // update global variable
        temp = readout.temperature.toFixed(2);
        humd = readout.humidity.toFixed(2);
    }
```

In the preceding code, we have added a couple of node modules, as follows:

- rpi-dht-sensor: https://www.npmjs.com/package/rpi-dht-sensor; this module will help us in reading the values of the DHT11 sensor
- rpio: https://www.npmjs.com/package/rpio; this module will help us manage GPIOs on the board, using which we will manage the LED

We have written a setInterval() that keeps running forever, every 3 seconds. Inside the callback, we call the getDHT11Values() that read the temperature and humidity from the sensor. If there is any change in the temperature and humidity values, we publish this data to the broker.

Also, notice the client.on('message'); here, we have added another if condition and are listening for the LED topic. If the current message is from the LED topic, we know that we will receive either a 1 or 0 indicating to switch on or switch off the LED.

Now, finally we will install the two modules, run:

```
npm install rpi-dht-sensor -save
npm install rpio -save
```

Save all the files and run npm start; this should connect the Raspberry Pi to the broker and subscribe to the LED topic, as follows:

```
[→ broker mosca -c index.js -v | pino
      +++.+++:    ,+++     +++;   '+++    +++.
     ++.+++.++    ++.++  ++,'+  `+',++  ++,++
     +`  +,  +: .+  .+  +;  +;  '+ '+  +`  +`
     +`  +.  +: ,+  `+  ++  +;  '+ ;+  +   +.
     +`  +.  +: ,+  `+  +'   '+      +   +.
     +`  +.  +: ,+  `+  :+.   '+      +++++.
     +`  +.  +: ,+  `+   ++   '+      +++++.
     +`  +.  +: ,+  `+   ++   '+      +   +.
     +`  +.  +: ,+  `+  +:  +:  '+ ;+  +   +.
     +`  +.  +: .+  .+  +;  +;  '+ '+  +   +.
     +`  +.  +: ++;++  ++'++   ++'+'  +   +.
     +`  +.  +:  +++   +++.  ,++'   +   +.
[2017-05-20T08:04:55.600Z] INFO (iotjs/22822 on Arvinds-MacBook-Pro.local): server started
    mqtts: 8883
[2017-05-20T08:04:56.388Z] INFO (iotjs/22822 on Arvinds-MacBook-Pro.local): client connected
    client: "rPI_3"
[2017-05-20T08:04:56.435Z] INFO (iotjs/22822 on Arvinds-MacBook-Pro.local): subscribed to topic
    topic: "rpi"
    qos: 0
    client: "rPI_3"
[2017-05-20T08:04:56.435Z] INFO (iotjs/22822 on Arvinds-MacBook-Pro.local): subscribed to topic
    topic: "led"
    qos: 0
    client: "rPI_3"
```

Additionally, if we see the console out from the Raspberry Pi, we should see something as follows:

Whenever there is a change in the data, the data is published to the broker. We have not yet implemented the logic for reacting to this data on the API engine, which we will do in the next section.

Updating the API engine

Now, we will add the required code to the MQTT client running on the API engine to handle the data from the device. Update `api-engine/server/mqtt/index.js`, as follows:

```javascript
var Data = require('../api/data/data.model');
var mqtt = require('mqtt');
var config = require('../config/environment');

var client = mqtt.connect({
    port: config.mqtt.port,
    protocol: 'mqtts',
    host: config.mqtt.host,
    clientId: config.mqtt.clientId,
    reconnectPeriod: 1000,
    username: config.mqtt.clientId,
    password: config.mqtt.clientId,
    keepalive: 300,
    rejectUnauthorized: false
});

client.on('connect', function() {
    console.log('Connected to Mosca at ' + config.mqtt.host + ' on port ' +
config.mqtt.port);
    client.subscribe('api-engine');
    client.subscribe('dht11');
});

client.on('message', function(topic, message) {
    // message is Buffer
    // console.log('Topic >> ', topic);
    // console.log('Message >> ', message.toString());
    if (topic === 'api-engine') {
        var macAddress = message.toString();
        console.log('Mac Address >> ', macAddress);
        client.publish('rpi', 'Got Mac Address: ' + macAddress);
    } else if (topic === 'dht11') {
        var data = JSON.parse(message.toString());
        // create a new data record for the device
        Data.create(data, function(err, data) {
```

```
            if (err) return console.error(err);
            // if the record has been saved successfully,
            // websockets will trigger a message to the web-app
            console.log('Data Saved :', data.data);
        });
    } else {
        console.log('Unknown topic', topic);
    }
});

exports.sendLEDData = function(data) {
    console.log('Sending Data', data);
    client.publish('led', data);
}
```

Here, we have subscribed to a topic named dht11, to listen for a message published by the Raspberry Pi about the temperature and humidity values. We have also exposed another method named sendLEDData that will accept the data that needs to be sent to the device.

If we save all the files and restart the API engine, we should see something as follows:

```
[→  api-engine npm start

> api-engine@0.1.0 start /Users/arvindravulavaru/Arvind/Books/Advanced IoT with JS/code/chapter2/api-engine
> nodemon server/app.js

[nodemon] 1.11.0
[nodemon] to restart at any time, enter `rs`
[nodemon] watching: *.*
[nodemon] starting `node server/app.js`
Express server listening on 9000, in development mode
Connected to Mosca at 127.0.0.1 on port 8883
Mac Address >>  b8:27:eb:39:92:0d
[iMjmlGqKGLvrOdVsAAAA] Connected on 127.0.0.1
Data Saved : { t: '25.00', h: '31.00', l: 0 }
Data Saved : { t: '26.00', h: '31.00', l: 0 }
```

From the preceding screenshot, we can see that the data comes from the Raspberry Pi and gets saved to MongoDB. To validate if the data is saved, we can head over to the `mlab` DB and look for a collection named `datas` and it should look as follows:

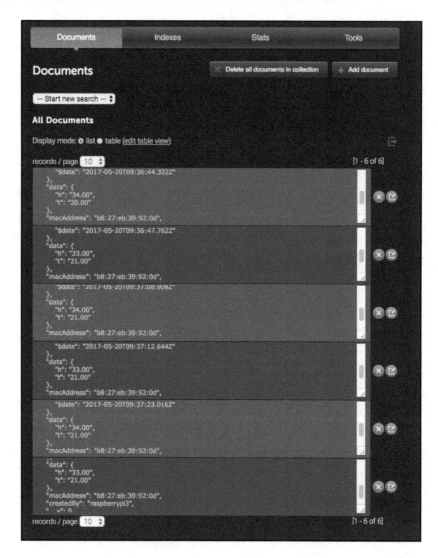

Whenever the data is saved successfully, the same copy will be sent to the web app as well. In the next section, we will display this data in real time on the web dashboard.

Updating the web app

In this section, we will develop the code needed to display the data in real time inside the web app, as well as provide an interface, using which we can turn on/off the LED.

We will get started by adding a toggle switch component. We will use the ngx-ui-switch (https://github.com/webcat12345/ngx-ui-switch) for the same.

From inside the web-app-base folder, run the following command:

```
npm install ngx-ui-switch -save
```

We will use the ng2-charts https://valor-software.com/ng2-charts/ for plotting charts of our temperature and humidity values. We will install this module as well by running the following command:

```
npm install ng2-charts --save
npm install chart.js --save
```

This will install the toggle switch and ng2-charts modules. Next, we need to add this to @NgModule. Open web-app/src/app/app.module.ts and add the following command to the imports:

```
import { UiSwitchModule } from 'ngx-ui-switch';
import { ChartsModule } from 'ng2-charts';
```

Then, add UiSwitchModule and ChartsModule to the imports array:

```
// snipp snipp
imports: [
    RouterModule.forRoot(appRoutes),
    BrowserModule,
    BrowserAnimationsModule,
    FormsModule,
    HttpModule,
    LocalStorageModule.withConfig({
      prefix: 'web-app',
      storageType: 'localStorage'
    }),
    SimpleNotificationsModule.forRoot(),
    UiSwitchModule,
    ChartsModule
  ],
// snipp snipp
```

Once this is done, we need to import `chart.js` into our application. Open `web-app/.angular-cli.json` and update the `scripts` section, as follows:

```
// snipp snipp
"scripts": [
        "../node_modules/chart.js/dist/Chart.js"
    ],
// snipp snipp
```

Save all the files and restart the web app, if it is already running.

Now, we can use this directive in the device component.

In our current use case, we have to display the temperature and humidity values as well as provide a toggle switch to turn the LED on/off. For this, our template in `web-app/src/app/device/device.component.html` will be as follows:

```
<div class="container">
    <br>
    <div *ngIf="!device">
        <h3 class="text-center">Loading!</h3>
    </div>
    <div class="row" *ngIf="lastRecord">
        <div class="col-md-12">
            <div class="panel panel-info">
                <div class="panel-heading">
                    <h3 class="panel-title">
                        {{device.name}}
                    </h3>
                    <span class="pull-right btn-click">
                        <i class="fa fa-chevron-circle-up"></i>
                    </span>
                </div>
                <div class="clearfix"></div>
                <div class="table-responsive">
                    <table class="table table-striped">
                        <tr>
                            <td>Toggle LED</td>
                            <td>
                                <ui-switch [(ngModel)]="toggleState"
(change)="toggleChange($event)"></ui-switch>
                            </td>
                        </tr>
                        <tr *ngIf="lastRecord">
                            <td>Temperature</td>
                            <td>{{lastRecord.data.t}}</td>
                        </tr>
```

```html
                <tr *ngIf="lastRecord">
                    <td>Humidity</td>
                    <td>{{lastRecord.data.h}}</td>
                </tr>
                <tr *ngIf="lastRecord">
                    <td>Received At</td>
                    <td>{{lastRecord.createdAt | date:
'medium'}}</td>
                </tr>
            </table>
            <div class="col-md-10 col-md-offset-1"
*ngIf="lineChartData.length > 0">
                <canvas baseChart [datasets]="lineChartData"
[labels]="lineChartLabels" [options]="lineChartOptions"
[legend]="lineChartLegend" [chartType]="lineChartType"></canvas>
            </div>
        </div>
      </div>
    </div>
  </div>
</div>
```

The required code for the `DeviceComponent` class: `web-app/src/app/device/device.component.ts` will be as follows:

```typescript
import { Component, OnInit, OnDestroy } from '@angular/core';
import { DevicesService } from '../services/devices.service';
import { Params, ActivatedRoute } from '@angular/router';
import { SocketService } from '../services/socket.service';
import { DataService } from '../services/data.service';
import { NotificationsService } from 'angular2-notifications';

@Component({
    selector: 'app-device',
    templateUrl: './device.component.html',
    styleUrls: ['./device.component.css']
})
export class DeviceComponent implements OnInit, OnDestroy {
    device: any;
    data: Array<any>;
    toggleState: boolean = false;
    private subDevice: any;
    private subData: any;
    lastRecord: any;

    // line chart config
    public lineChartOptions: any = {
```

```
                responsive: true,
                legend: {
                        position: 'bottom',
                }, hover: {
                        mode: 'label'
                }, scales: {
                        xAxes: [{
                                display: true,
                                scaleLabel: {
                                        display: true,
                                        labelString: 'Time'
                                }
                        }],
                        yAxes: [{
                                display: true,
                                ticks: {
                                        beginAtZero: true,
                                        steps: 10,
                                        stepValue: 5,
                                        max: 70
                                }
                        }]
                },
                title: {
                        display: true,
                        text: 'Temperature & Humidity vs. Time'
                }
        };
        public lineChartLegend: boolean = true;
        public lineChartType: string = 'line';
        public lineChartData: Array<any> = [];
        public lineChartLabels: Array<any> = [];

        constructor(private deviceService: DevicesService,
                private socketService: SocketService,
                private dataService: DataService,
                private route: ActivatedRoute,
                private notificationsService: NotificationsService) { }

        ngOnInit() {
                this.subDevice = this.route.params.subscribe((params) => {
                        this.deviceService.getOne(params['id']).subscribe((response)
    => {
                                this.device = response.json();
                                this.getData();
                                this.socketInit();
                        });
                });
```

```
    }

    getData() {
        this.dataService.get(this.device.macAddress).subscribe((response)
=> {
            this.data = response.json();
            this.genChart();
            this.lastRecord = this.data[0]; // descending order data
            if (this.lastRecord) {
                this.toggleState = this.lastRecord.data.l;
            }
        });
    }

    toggleChange(state) {
        let data = {
            macAddress: this.device.macAddress,
            data: {
                t: this.lastRecord.data.t,
                h: this.lastRecord.data.h,
                l: state ? 1 : 0
            },
            topic: 'led'
        }

        this.dataService.create(data).subscribe((resp) => {
            if (resp.json()._id) {
                this.notificationsService.success('Device Notified!');
            }
        }, (err) => {
            console.log(err);
            this.notificationsService.error('Device Notification Failed.
Check console for the error!');
        })
    }

    socketInit() {
        this.subData =
this.socketService.getData(this.device.macAddress).subscribe((data) => {
            if(this.data.length <= 0) return;
            this.data.splice(this.data.length - 1, 1); // remove the
last record
            this.data.push(data); // add the new one
            this.lastRecord = data;
            this.genChart();
        });
    }
```

```
ngOnDestroy() {
        this.subDevice.unsubscribe();
        this.subData ? this.subData.unsubscribe() : '';
}

genChart() {

        let data = this.data;
        let _dtArr: Array<any> = [];
        let _lblArr: Array<any> = [];

        let tmpArr: Array<any> = [];
        let humArr: Array<any> = [];

        for (var i = 0; i < data.length; i++) {
                let _d = data[i];
                tmpArr.push(_d.data.t);
                humArr.push(_d.data.h);
                _lblArr.push(this.formatDate(_d.createdAt));
        }

        // reverse data to show the latest on the right side
        tmpArr.reverse();
        humArr.reverse();
        _lblArr.reverse();

        _dtArr = [
                {
                        data: tmpArr,
                        label: 'Temperature'
                },
                {
                        data: humArr,
                        label: 'Humidity %'
                },
        ]

        this.lineChartData = _dtArr;
        this.lineChartLabels = _lblArr;
}

private formatDate(originalTime) {
        var d = new Date(originalTime);
        var datestring = d.getDate() + "-" + (d.getMonth() + 1) + "-" +
d.getFullYear() + " " +
                d.getHours() + ":" + d.getMinutes();
        return datestring;
```

```
        }
    }
```

The key methods to notice are as follows:

- getData(): This method is used to get the last 30 records on page load. We are sending the data in the descending order from the API engine; hence we extract the last record and save it as the last record. We can use the remaining records to plot a chart if needed
- toggleChange(): This method will get fired when the toggle switch is clicked. This method will send the data to the API engine to save it
- socketInit(): This method keeps listening to the data save event on the device. Using this, we update the lastRecord variable with the latest data from the device
- genChart(): This method takes the data collection and then plots a graph. When a new data arrives over the socket, we remove the last record in the data array and push the new record, keeping the total size of 30 records at all times

With this, we are done with the development of the template needed to process this setup.

Save all files, launch the broker, API engine, and the web app and then log in to the application and then navigate to the device page.

If everything is set up correctly, we should see the following screen:

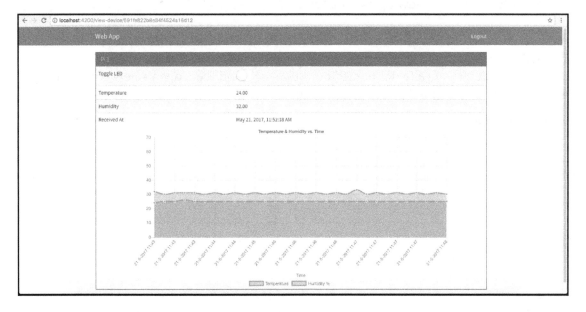

Now, whenever the data comes via sockets, the chart updates automatically!

Now to test the LED, toggle the **LED** button to on and you should see that the LED that we have set up on the Raspberry Pi will light up and similarly if we turn it off, it will turn off the LED.

Building the desktop app and implementing an end-to-end flow

Now that we are done with an end-to-end flow with the web app, we will extend the same to the desktop and mobile apps. We will start off by building a desktop client for the same API engine. So, if a user is more comfortable in using a desktop app over a web or mobile app, he/she could use this.

This desktop app, we will have all the same features as the web app.

For building the desktop app, we will use the electron (`https://electron.atom.io/`) framework. Using a Yeoman (`http://yeoman.io/`) generator named `generator-electron` (`https://github.com/sindresorhus/generator-electron`), we will scaffold the base application. Then, we will build our web app and use the `dist` folder from that build as an input to the desktop app. All this will be more clear once we start working.

To get started, run the following command:

```
npm install yo generator-electron -g
```

This will install the yeoman generator and the electron generator. Next, inside the `chapter2` folder, create a folder named `desktop-app` and then, open a new command prompt/terminal and run the following command:

```
yo electron
```

This wizard will ask a few questions and you can answer them accordingly:

```
[? What do you want to name your app? desktop-app
[? What is your GitHub username? arvindr21
[? What is the URL of your website? https://github.com/arvindr21
   create package.json
   create index.css
   create index.html
   create index.js
   create license
   create readme.md
   create .editorconfig
   create .gitattributes
   create .gitignore


I'm all done. Running npm install for you to install the required dependencies. If this fails, try running the command yourself.
```

This will go ahead and install the required dependencies. Once the installation is completed, we should see a folder structure, as follows:

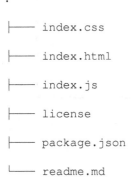

With the `node_modules` folder present at the root.

Everything starts with `desktop-app/package.json` start script, which launches the `desktop-app/index.js`. `desktop-app/index.js` creates a new browser window and launches the `desktop-app/index.html` page.

To quickly test drive from inside the `desktop-app` folder, run the following command:

```
npm start
```

As a result, we should see the following screen:

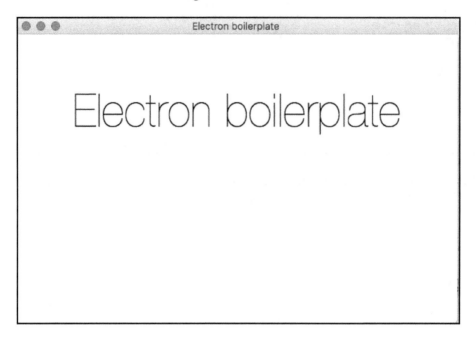

Now, we will add the required code. At the root of the `desktop-app` folder, create a file named `freeport.js` and update `desktop-app/freeport.js`, as follows:

```javascript
var net = require('net')
module.exports = function(cb) {
    var server = net.createServer(),
        port = 0;
    server.on('listening', function() {
        port = server.address().port
        server.close()
    });
    server.on('close', function() {
        cb(null, port)
    })
    server.on('error', function(err) {
        cb(err, null)
    })
    server.listen(0, '127.0.0.1')
}
```

With the preceding code, we will find a free port on the end user's machine and launch our web app inside the electron shell.

Next, create a folder named `app` at the root of the `desktop-app` folder. We will dump files into this in a moment. Next, at the root of the `desktop-app` folder, create a file named `server.js`. Update `server.js`, as follows:

```
var FreePort = require('./freeport.js');
var http = require('http'),
    fs = require('fs'),
    html = '';

module.exports = function(cb) {
    FreePort(function(err, port) {
        console.log(port);
        http.createServer(function(request, response) {
            if (request.url === '/') {
                html = fs.readFileSync('./app/index.html');
            } else {
                html = fs.readFileSync('./app' + request.url);
            }
            response.writeHeader(200, { "Content-Type": "text/html" });
            response.write(html);
            response.end();
        }).listen(port);
        cb(port);
    });
}
```

Here, we listen to a free port and launch `index.html`. Now, all we need to do is update `createMainWindow()` in `desktop-app/index.js`, as follows:

```
// snipp snipp
function createMainWindow() {
    const { width, height } =
electron.screen.getPrimaryDisplay().workAreaSize;
    const win = new electron.BrowserWindow({ width, height })
    const server = require("./server")(function(port) {
        win.loadURL('http://localhost:' + port);
        win.on('closed', onClosed);
        console.log('Desktop app started on port :', port);
    });

    return win;
}
// snipp snipp
```

That is all the setup we need.

Now, head back to the terminal/prompt of the web-app folder (yes web-app, not desktop-app) and run the following command:

ng build --env=prod

This will create a new folder inside the web app folder named dist. The contents of the dist folder should be on the following lines:

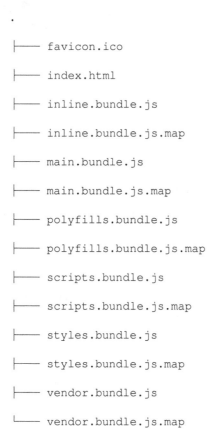

```
.
├── favicon.ico
├── index.html
├── inline.bundle.js
├── inline.bundle.js.map
├── main.bundle.js
├── main.bundle.js.map
├── polyfills.bundle.js
├── polyfills.bundle.js.map
├── scripts.bundle.js
├── scripts.bundle.js.map
├── styles.bundle.js
├── styles.bundle.js.map
├── vendor.bundle.js
└── vendor.bundle.js.map
```

All code we have written in the web app is finally bundled into the preceding files. We will grab all the files (not the `dist` folder) present inside the `dist` folder and then paste it inside the `desktop-app/app` folder. The final structure of the desktop app after the preceding changes will be as follows:

```
.

├── app
│   ├── favicon.ico
│   ├── index.html
│   ├── inline.bundle.js
│   ├── inline.bundle.js.map
│   ├── main.bundle.js
│   ├── main.bundle.js.map
│   ├── polyfills.bundle.js
│   ├── polyfills.bundle.js.map
│   ├── scripts.bundle.js
│   ├── scripts.bundle.js.map
│   ├── styles.bundle.js
│   ├── styles.bundle.js.map
│   ├── vendor.bundle.js
│   └── vendor.bundle.js.map
├── freeport.js
├── index.css
├── index.html
├── index.js
├── license
```

```
├──── package.json

├──── readme.md

└──── server.js
```

From now on, we are just going to paste the contents of the `web-app/dist` folder into the `app` folder of the `desktop-app`.

To test drive, run the following command:

npm start

This will bring up the log in screen, as follows:

If you see a pop up as shown previously, allow it. Once you have successfully logged in, you should be able to see all the devices in your account, as follows:

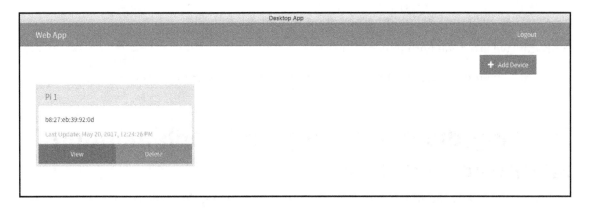

And finally, the device information screen:

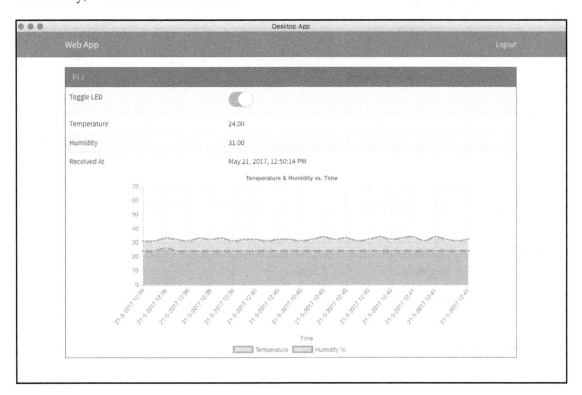

Now we can turn the LED on/off and it should react accordingly.

With this, we are done with the desktop app.

In the next section, we will build a mobile app using the Ionic framework.

Building the mobile app and implementing an end-to-end flow

In this section, we will build our mobile companion app using the Ionic framework (http://ionicframework.com/). The output or the example would be the same as what we have done for the web and desktop app.

To get started, we will install the latest version of ionic and cordova by running the following command:

```
npm install -g ionic cordova
```

Now, we need the mobile app base. If you have not already cloned the book's code repository, you can do so using the following command (anywhere on your machine):

```
git clone git@github.com:PacktPublishing/Practical-Internet-of-Things-with-JavaScript.git
```

or you can download the zip file from https://github.com/PacktPublishing/Practical-Internet-of-Things-with-JavaScript as well.

Once the repository has been downloaded, cd into the base folder and make a copy of mobile-app-base folder into chapter2 folder.

Once the copy is completed, cd into the mobile-app folder and run the following command:

```
npm install
```

And then

```
ionic cordova platform add android
```

Or

```
ionic cordova platform add ios
```

This will take care of installing the required dependencies and adding Android or iOS platforms.

If we look at the `mobile-app` folder, we should see the following:

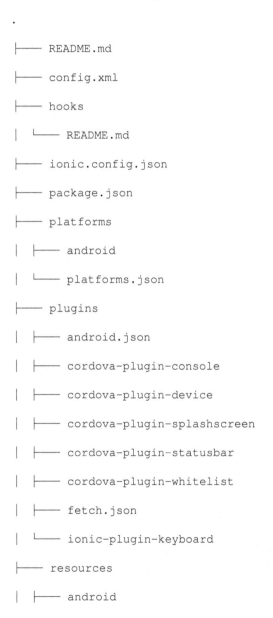

```
.

├─── README.md

├─── config.xml

├─── hooks

│    └─── README.md

├─── ionic.config.json

├─── package.json

├─── platforms

│    ├─── android

│    └─── platforms.json

├─── plugins

│    ├─── android.json

│    ├─── cordova-plugin-console

│    ├─── cordova-plugin-device

│    ├─── cordova-plugin-splashscreen

│    ├─── cordova-plugin-statusbar

│    ├─── cordova-plugin-whitelist

│    ├─── fetch.json

│    └─── ionic-plugin-keyboard

├─── resources

│    ├─── android
```

```
|   ├── icon.png
|   ├── ios
|   └── splash.png
├── src
|   ├── app
|   ├── assets
|   ├── declarations.d.ts
|   ├── index.html
|   ├── manifest.json
|   ├── pages
|   ├── service-worker.js
|   ├── services
|   └── theme
├── tsconfig.json
├── tslint.json
└── www
├── assets
├── build
├── index.html
├── manifest.json
└── service-worker.js
```

In our `mobile-app` folder, the most important file is `mobile-app/config.xml`. This file consists of the definitions needed by cordova to convert the HTML/CSS/JS application into a hybrid mobile app.

Next, we have the `mobile-app/resources`, `mobile-app/plugins`, and `mobile-app/platforms` folder that will consist of the cordova wrapped code for the app we are developing.

And finally, the `mobile-app/src` folder, this folder is where we have all our source code. The setup for the mobile is similar to what we had for the web app and the desktop app. We have a service folder that has the `mobile-app/src/services/auth.service.ts` for authentication, `mobile-app/src/services/device.service.ts` for interfacing with the devices API, `mobile-app/src/services/data.service.ts` for fetching the latest data from the device, `mobile-app/src/services/socket.service.ts` to set up web sockets in our mobile app, and finally, `mobile-app/src/services/toast.service.ts` to show notifications, tailored to a mobile. `mobile-app/src/services/toast.service.ts` is similar to the notification service we have used in the web and desktop apps.

Next, we have the needed pages. The mobile app implements only the login page. We are forcing the user to use the web or desktop app to create a new account. `mobile-app/src/pages/login/login.ts` consists of the authentication logic. `mobile-app/src/pages/home/home.ts` consists of the list of all devices that a user is registered with. `mobile-app/src/pages/add-device/add-device.ts` has the logic needed to add a new device and `mobile-app/src/pages/view-device/view-device.ts` to view the device information.

Now, from inside the `mobile-app` folder, run the following command:

```
ionic serve
```

This will launch the app in the browser. If you would like to test it on an actual app, you can run the following command:

```
ionic cordova run android
```

Alternatively, you can run the following command:

```
ionic cordova run ios
```

This will launch the app on the device. In either case, the app will behave the same.

Once the app is launched, we will see the login page:

Once we have successfully logged in, we should see the home page as follows. We can add a new device using the + icon in the header:

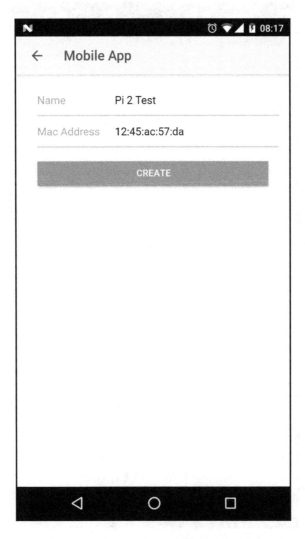

The newly created device should reflect on our home screen, as follows:

If we click on **VIEW DEVICE**, we should see the device information, as follows:

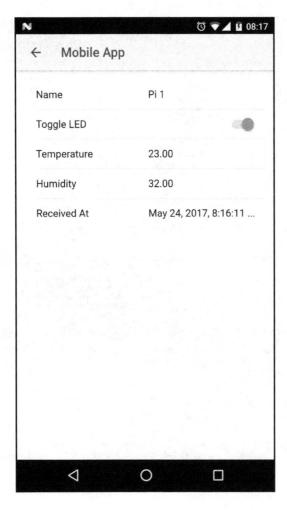

When we toggle the button on/off, the LED on the Raspberry Pi should turn on/off:

Another view of the same setup is shown as follows:

The preceding is the setup of the Raspberry Pi 3 with a DHT11 sensor and LED.

With this, we have successfully established an end-to-end architecture for executing out the Internet of Things examples. From now on, we will work with the web app, mobile app, desktop app, Raspberry Pi, and a bit of API engine for our next examples. The changes we will make are minimal. We will focus on the use case rather than building the setup again and again.

Troubleshooting

In case you do not see the expected output, check the following:

- Check if the broker, API engine, web app, and Raspberry Pi app are running
- Check the IP address of the broker provided to the Raspberry Pi
- Check the IP address of the API engine provided to the mobile app

Summary

In Chapter 2, *IoTFW.js - I* and in this chapter, we went through the entire process of setting up an entire frame to work with the Internet of Things solutions. We built the entire framework using only JavaScript as our programming language.

We started with understanding the architecture and data flow from Raspberry Pi to an end user device, such as a web app, desktop app, or a mobile app. Then we started working on the broker using Mosca, after setting up MongoDB. Next we designed and developed the API engine and completed the basic Raspberry Pi setup.

We worked on the web app and desktop app and integrated a simple LED and a DHT11 temperature and humidity sensor with the Raspberry Pi, and saw a simple flow from one end to another. We streamed the temperature and humidity in real time to the web app and desktop app, and using the toggle button, we turned on the LED.

And finally, we built a mobile app and implemented/validated the LED and DHT11 setup.

In the Chapter 4, *Smart Agriculture*, using the current setup as a base, we will build a smart agriculture solution.

4
Smart Agriculture

In this chapter, we are going to take our framework which we built in Chapter 2, *IoTFW.js - I* and Chapter 3, *IoTFW.js - II,* and start working on various use cases. We are going to start with the agricultural sector and build a smart weather station in this chapter.

A simple requirement for any farmer is to have the ability to understand the environmental factors near and around their farm. So, we are going to build a prototype of a portable weather station. We are going to work on the following topics in this chapter:

- Agriculture and IoT
- Designing a smart weather station
- Developing the code for Raspberry Pi 3
- Updating MQTT code in the API engine
- Modifying the templates for web apps, desktop apps, and mobile apps

Agriculture and IoT

A report by Beecham Research predicts that the world population will reach 8 billion by 2025 and 9.6 billion by 2050, and in order to keep pace, food production must increase by 70% by 2050. Here is the report:
https://www.beechamresearch.com/files/BRL%20Smart%20Farming%20Executive%20Summary.pdf

This means that we need to find quicker and more productive ways of farming. Land and resources are going to get scarcer as we keep moving toward 2050. This is when, given the resources, we would need to feed more mouths than ever before, unless a zombie apocalypse comes and all of us get eaten up by other zombies!

This is a very good opportunity for technology to provide solutions to make this happen. IoT has almost always been about smart homes, smart offices, and convenience, but it can do more than that. That is what we are going to cover in this chapter. We are going to build a smart weather station that a farmer can deploy in their farm to get real-time metrics such as temperature, humidity, soil moisture, and rain detection.

Other sensors can be added based on availability and need.

Designing a smart weather station

Now that we have an idea of what we are building and why, let us get started with the design. The first thing we are going to do is identify the sensors needed. In this smart weather station, we are going to use the following:

- A temperature sensor
- A humidity sensor
- A soil moisture sensor
- A rain detector sensor

I have picked sensors that are available off the shelf, to showcase the proof of concept. Most of them will work well for testing, and validating an idea, or as a hobby, but are not suitable for production.

We are going to connect these sensors to our Raspberry Pi 3. We are going to use the following models for the sensors:

- Temperature and humidity:
  https://www.amazon.com/Gowoops-Temperature-Humidity-Digital-Raspberry/dp/B01H3J3H82/ref=sr_1_5
- Soil moisture sensor:
  https://www.amazon.com/Hygrometer-Humidity-Detection-Moisture-Arduino/dp/B01FDGUHBM/ref=sr_1_4
- Rain detector sensor:
  https://www.amazon.com/Uxcell-a13082300ux1431-Rainwater-Detection-3-3V-5V/dp/B00GN7O7JE

You can buy these sensors elsewhere as well.

As we have seen in `Chapter 3`, *IoTFW.js - II*, the temperature and humidity sensor is a digital sensor, and we are going to use the `node-dht-sensor` module to read the temperature and humidity values. The soil moisture sensor is an analog sensor, and Raspberry Pi 3 does not have any analog pins. For this, we are going to use a 12-bit A/D IC from Microchip named MCP3208, to convert the analog output from the sensor and feed it to Raspberry Pi over the SPI protocol.

Wikipedia defines the SPI protocol in the following way:

> *The **Serial Peripheral Interface (SPI)** bus is a synchronous serial communication interface specification used for short distance communication, primarily in embedded systems. The interface was developed by Motorola in the late 1980s and has become a de facto standard.*

 For more information on SPI, refer to: `https://en.wikipedia.org/wiki/Serial_Peripheral_Interface_Bus`.

The rain detector sensor can be read as both analog and digital. We are going to use the analog output to detect the level of rain, and not just whether it is raining or not.

Going back to MCP3208, it is a 16-pin package that can read eight analog inputs at once and can convert them and feed to Raspberry Pi over the SPI protocol. You can read more about MCP3208 IC here: `http://ww1.microchip.com/downloads/en/DeviceDoc/21298c.pdf`. You can purchase it from here: `https://www.amazon.com/Adafruit-MCP3008-8-Channel-Interface-Raspberry/dp/B00NAY3RB2/ref=sr_1_1`.

We are going to connect the temperature and humidity sensor directly to Raspberry Pi 3, and the moisture sensor and the rain sensor to MCP3208, and MCP3208 will connect to Raspberry Pi 3 over SPI.

And on the broker, we are not going to change anything. In the API engine, we are going to add a new topic to the MQTT client named `weather-status`, and then send the data from Raspberry Pi 3 to this topic.

On the web app, we are going to update the template for viewing the weather metrics. The same goes for the desktop app and mobile app.

Setting up Raspberry Pi 3

Let us get started with the schematics.

Set up Raspberry Pi 3 and the sensors as shown here:

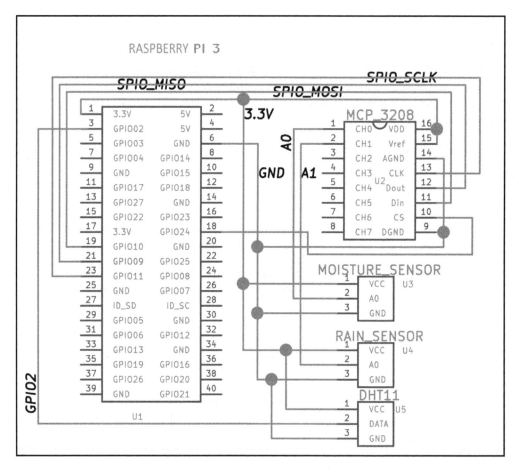

Here is a table showing these connections:

Raspberry Pi and MCP3208

Refer to the following table:

Raspberry Pi pin number - pin name	MCP3208 pin number - pin name
1 - 3.3V	16 - VDD
1 - 3.3V	15 - AREF
6 - GND	14 - AGND
23 - GPIO11, SPI0_SCLK	13 - CLK
21 - GPIO09, SPI0_MISO	12 - DOUT
19 -GPIO10, SPI0_MOSI	11 - DIN
24 - GPIO08, CEO	10 - CS
6 - GND	9 - DGND

Moisture sensor and MCP3208

Refer to the following table:

MCP3208 pin number - pin name	Sensor name - pin number
1 - A0	Rain sensor - A0
2 - A1	Moisture sensor - A0

Raspberry Pi and DHT11

Refer to the following table:

Raspberry Pi number - pin name	Sensor name - pin number
3 - GPIO2	DHT11 - Data

All grounds and all 3.3V are connected to a common point.

Once we have connected the sensors as shown previously, we will write the code needed to interface with the sensors.

Before we go further, we are going to copy the entire Chapter 2, *IoTFW.js - I*, and Chapter 3, *IoTFW.js - II*, code into another folder named chapter4.

The chapter4 folder should look as shown here:

```
.
├── api-engine
│   ├── package.json
│   └── server
├── broker
│   ├── certs
│   └── index.js
├── desktop-app
│   ├── app
│   ├── freeport.js
│   ├── index.css
│   ├── index.html
│   ├── index.js
│   ├── license
│   ├── package.json
│   ├── readme.md
│   └── server.js
├── mobile-app
│   ├── config.xml
│   ├── hooks
```

```
|   ├──── ionic.config.json
|   ├──── package.json
|   ├──── platforms
|   ├──── plugins
|   ├──── resources
|   ├──── src
|   ├──── tsconfig.json
|   ├──── tslint.json
|   └──── www
└──── web-app
├──── README.md
├──── e2e
├──── karma.conf.js
├──── package.json
├──── protractor.conf.js
├──── src
├──── tsconfig.json
└──── tslint.json
```

We will head back to the Raspberry Pi and inside the `pi-client` folder, we will update the `index.js` file. Update `pi-client/index.js`, as shown here:

```
var config = require('./config.js');

var mqtt = require('mqtt');

var GetMac = require('getmac');

var async = require('async');
```

```
var rpiDhtSensor = require('rpi-dht-sensor');

var McpAdc = require('mcp-adc');

var adc = new McpAdc.Mcp3208();

var dht11 = new rpiDhtSensor.DHT11(2);

var temp = 0,

prevTemp = 0;

var humd = 0,

prevHumd = 0;

var macAddress;

var state = 0;

var moistureVal = 0,

prevMoistureVal = 0;

var rainVal = 0,

prevRainVal = 0;

var client = mqtt.connect({

port: config.mqtt.port,

protocol: 'mqtts',

host: config.mqtt.host,

clientId: config.mqtt.clientId,

reconnectPeriod: 1000,

username: config.mqtt.clientId,

password: config.mqtt.clientId,

keepalive: 300,

rejectUnauthorized: false
```

```
});

client.on('connect', function() {

client.subscribe('rpi');

GetMac.getMac(function(err, mac) {

if (err) throw err;

macAddress = mac;

client.publish('api-engine', mac);

});

});

client.on('message', function(topic, message) {

message = message.toString();

if (topic === 'rpi') {

console.log('API Engine Response >> ', message);

} else {

console.log('Unknown topic', topic);

}

});

// infinite loop, with 3 seconds delay

setInterval(function() {

readSensorValues(function(results) {

console.log('Temperature: ' + temp + 'C, ' + 'humidity: ' + humd + '%, ' +
' Rain level (%):' + rainVal + ', ' + 'moistureVal (%): ' + moistureVal);

// if the temperature and humidity values change

// then only publish the values

if (temp !== prevTemp || humd !== prevHumd || moistureVal !==
```

```
prevMoistureVal || rainVal != prevRainVal) {

var data2Send = {

data: {

t: temp,

h: humd,

r: rainVal,

m: moistureVal

},

macAddress: macAddress

};

// console.log('Data Published');

client.publish('weather-status', JSON.stringify(data2Send));

// reset prev values to current

// for next loop

prevTemp = temp;

prevHumd = humd;

prevMoistureVal = moistureVal;

prevRainVal = rainVal;

}

});

}, 3000); // every three second

// `CB` expects {

// dht11Values: val,

// rainLevel: val,
```

```
// moistureLevel: val

// }

function readSensorValues(CB) {

async.parallel({

dht11Values: function(callback) {

var readout = dht11.read();

// update global variable

temp = readout.temperature.toFixed(2);

humd = readout.humidity.toFixed(2);

callback(null, { temp: temp, humidity: humd });

},

rainLevel: function(callback) {

// we are going to connect rain sensor

// on channel 0, hence 0 is the first arg below

adc.readRawValue(0, function(value) {

// update global variable

rainVal = value;

rainVal = (100 - parseFloat((rainVal / 4096) * 100)).toFixed(2);

callback(null, { rain: rainVal });

});

},

moistureLevel: function(callback) {

// we are going to connect moisture sensor

// on channel 1, hence 1 is the first arg below
```

```
adc.readRawValue(1, function(value) {

// update global variable

moistureVal = value;

moistureVal = (100 - parseFloat((moistureVal / 4096) * 100)).toFixed(2);

callback(null, { moisture: moistureVal });

});

}

}, function done(err, results) {

if (err) {

throw err;

}

// console.log(results);

if (CB) CB(results);

});

}
```

In the preceding code, we have left the MQTT setup as is. We have added the `mcp-adc` (`https://github.com/anha1/mcp-adc`) and `async` (`https://github.com/caolan/async`) modules. `mcp-adc` manages the SPI protocol interface exposed by MCP3208, and we are using the `async` module to read data from all sensors in parallel.

We have started off by establishing a connection with the broker over MQTTS. Then, we have set up an infinite loop using `setInterval()` with a time delay of 3 seconds between executions. Inside the `callback` of `setInterval()`, we have invoked `readSensorValues()` to get the latest sensor values.

`readSensorValues()` uses `async.parallel()` to read the three sensors in parallel and update the data in the global variables we have defined. Once all the sensor data is gathered, we are passing the results to the `callback` function as an argument.

Once we receive the sensor data, we are going to check whether something has changed between the temperature, humidity, rain, and moisture values. If nothing has changed, we chill; otherwise, we will publish this data to the broker on the weather-status topic.

Save all the files. Now, we will start the Mosca broker from our desktop machine:

```
mosca -c index.js -v | pino
```

Once you have started the Mosca server, check the IP address of the server on which Mosca is running. Update the same IP in your Raspberry Pi `config.js` file. Otherwise, Raspberry Pi cannot post data to the broker.

Once Mosca has started successfully and we have validated the IP, run this on Raspberry Pi:

```
sudo node index.js
```

This will start the server, and we should see the following:

```
pi@raspberrypi: ~/Desktop/pi-client
File  Edit  Tabs  Help
pi@raspberrypi:~/Desktop/pi-client $ sudo node index.js
{ MODE: { MODE_0: 0, MODE_1: 1, MODE_2: 2, MODE_3: 3 },
  CS: { none: 64, high: 4, low: 0 },
  ORDER: { msb: false, lsb: true },
  Spi: [Function: Spi] }
Spi { _spi: _spi {}, device: '/dev/spidev0.0' }
API Engine Response >> Got Mac Address: b8:27:eb:39:92:0d
Temperature: 21.00C, humidity: 19.00%,  Rain level (%):1.86, mositureVal (%): 4.57
Temperature: 21.00C, humidity: 19.00%,  Rain level (%):1.78, mositureVal (%): 4.59
Temperature: 21.00C, humidity: 19.00%,  Rain level (%):99.83, mositureVal (%): 8.25
Temperature: 21.00C, humidity: 19.00%,  Rain level (%):99.80, mositureVal (%): 72.73
Temperature: 21.00C, humidity: 19.00%,  Rain level (%):99.73, mositureVal (%): 89.14
Temperature: 21.00C, humidity: 19.00%,  Rain level (%):99.83, mositureVal (%): 89.18
Temperature: 21.00C, humidity: 19.00%,  Rain level (%):98.07, mositureVal (%): 89.18
Temperature: 21.00C, humidity: 19.00%,  Rain level (%):96.46, mositureVal (%): 89.21
Temperature: 21.00C, humidity: 19.00%,  Rain level (%):96.95, mositureVal (%): 89.26
Temperature: 21.00C, humidity: 19.00%,  Rain level (%):97.29, mositureVal (%): 89.28
Temperature: 21.00C, humidity: 19.00%,  Rain level (%):97.53, mositureVal (%): 89.28
Temperature: 21.00C, humidity: 19.00%,  Rain level (%):97.75, mositureVal (%): 89.33
Temperature: 21.00C, humidity: 19.00%,  Rain level (%):97.92, mositureVal (%): 89.36
Temperature: 21.00C, humidity: 19.00%,  Rain level (%):98.07, mositureVal (%): 89.38
Temperature: 21.00C, humidity: 19.00%,  Rain level (%):98.22, mositureVal (%): 89.43
Temperature: 21.00C, humidity: 19.00%,  Rain level (%):98.34, mositureVal (%): 89.48
```

When I started the Raspberry Pi, the rain sensor was dry and the moisture sensor was placed inside dry soil. Initially, the value of the rain sensor was `1.86%` and the moisture sensor value was `4.57%`.

When I added water to the plant/moisture sensor, the percentage increased to `98.83%`; similarly, when I simulated rainfall on the rain sensor, the value went up to `89.48%`.

Here is my prototype setup of the smart weather station:

 The blue chip is DHT11, the moisture sensor is plotted inside my desk-side plant, and the rain sensor is placed inside a plastic tray for collecting rainwater. The breadboard has the MCP3208 IC and the required connections.

Lots of wires!

With this, we complete the code needed for Raspberry Pi 3. In the next section, we are going to set up the code needed for the API engine.

Setting up the API engine

In this last section, we have seen how to set up the components and code needed to set up our smart weather station using Raspberry Pi 3. Now, we will work on managing the data that we receive on the API engine from the Raspberry Pi 3.

Open `api-engine/server/mqtt/index.js` and update it, as shown here:

```
var Data = require('../api/data/data.model');
var mqtt = require('mqtt');
var config = require('../config/environment');

var client = mqtt.connect({
port: config.mqtt.port,
protocol: 'mqtts',
host: config.mqtt.host,
clientId: config.mqtt.clientId,
reconnectPeriod: 1000,
username: config.mqtt.clientId,
password: config.mqtt.clientId,
keepalive: 300,
rejectUnauthorized: false
});

client.on('connect', function() {
console.log('Connected to Mosca at ' + config.mqtt.host + ' on port ' +
config.mqtt.port);
client.subscribe('api-engine');
client.subscribe('weather-status');
});

client.on('message', function(topic, message) {
    // message is Buffer
    // console.log('Topic >> ', topic);
    // console.log('Message >> ', message.toString());
if (topic === 'api-engine') {
varmacAddress = message.toString();
console.log('Mac Address >> ', macAddress);
client.publish('rpi', 'Got Mac Address: ' + macAddress);
    } else if (topic === 'weather-status') {
```

```
var data = JSON.parse(message.toString());
        // create a new data record for the device
Data.create(data, function(err, data) {
if (err) return console.error(err);
            // if the record has been saved successfully,
            // websockets will trigger a message to the web-app
console.log('Data Saved :', data.data);
        });
    } else {
console.log('Unknown topic', topic);
    }
});
```

Here, we are waiting for a message on the `weather-status` topic, and when we receive the data from the Raspberry Pi, we save it to our database and that pushes the data to the web app, mobile app, and desktop app.

Those are all the changes we need to make to absorb the data from the Raspberry Pi 3 and pass it on to the web, desktop, and mobile apps.

Save all the files and run the following code:

npm start

This will start the API engine and connect to Mosca, along with Raspberry Pi:

```
[→ broker mosca -c index.js -v | pino
       +++.+++:    ,+++    +++;  '+++   +++.
      ++.+++.++   ++.++  ++,'+  `+',++  ++,++
     +`  +,  +: .+ .+  +; +; '+ '+  +`  +`
     +`  +,  +: ,+  `+  ++  +; '+ ;+  +   +.
     +`  +,  +: ,+  `+  +'   '+     +   +.
     +`  +,  +: ,+  `+  :+.   '+     +++++.
     +`  +,  +: ,+  `+   ++   '+     +++++.
     +`  +,  +: ,+  `+   ++   '+     +   +.
     +`  +,  +: ,+  `+ +: +: '+ ;+  +   +.
     +`  +,  +: .+ .+  +; +; '+ '+  +   +.
     +`  +,  +: ++;++  ++'++  ++'+'  +   +.
     +`  +,  +:  +++   +++.  ,++'    +   +.
[2017-06-10T07:59:02.128Z] INFO (iotjs/21105 on Arvinds-MacBook-Pro.local): server started
    mqtts: 8883
[2017-06-10T08:00:04.988Z] INFO (iotjs/21105 on Arvinds-MacBook-Pro.local): client connected
    client: "API_Server_Dev"
[2017-06-10T08:00:05.001Z] INFO (iotjs/21105 on Arvinds-MacBook-Pro.local): subscribed to topic
    topic: "api-engine"
    qos: 0
    client: "API_Server_Dev"
[2017-06-10T08:00:05.004Z] INFO (iotjs/21105 on Arvinds-MacBook-Pro.local): subscribed to topic
    topic: "weather-status"
    qos: 0
    client: "API_Server_Dev"
[2017-06-10T08:00:12.499Z] INFO (iotjs/21105 on Arvinds-MacBook-Pro.local): client connected
    client: "rPI_3"
[2017-06-10T08:00:12.747Z] INFO (iotjs/21105 on Arvinds-MacBook-Pro.local): subscribed to topic
    topic: "rpi"
    qos: 0
    client: "rPI_3"
```

And if we leave the API engine running for a while, we should see the following:

```
[→  api-engine npm start

> api-engine@0.1.0 start /Users/arvindravulavaru/Arvind/Books/Advanced IoT with JS/code/chapter4/api-engine
> nodemon server/app.js

[nodemon] 1.10.0
[nodemon] to restart at any time, enter `rs`
[nodemon] watching: *.*
[nodemon] starting `node server/app.js`
Express server listening on 9000, in development mode
Connected to Mosca at 127.0.0.1 on port 8883
[hatcFRcIgP8ZkIvrAAAA] Connected on 192.168.10.11
Mac Address >>  b8:27:eb:39:92:0d
Data Saved : { t: '21.00', h: '19.00', r: '1.86', m: '4.57' }
Data Saved : { t: '21.00', h: '19.00', r: '1.78', m: '4.59' }
Data Saved : { t: '21.00', h: '19.00', r: '99.83', m: '8.25' }
Data Saved : { t: '21.00', h: '19.00', r: '99.80', m: '72.73' }
Data Saved : { t: '21.00', h: '19.00', r: '99.73', m: '89.14' }
Data Saved : { t: '21.00', h: '19.00', r: '99.83', m: '89.18' }
Data Saved : { t: '21.00', h: '19.00', r: '98.07', m: '89.18' }
Data Saved : { t: '21.00', h: '19.00', r: '96.46', m: '89.21' }
Data Saved : { t: '21.00', h: '19.00', r: '96.95', m: '89.26' }
Data Saved : { t: '21.00', h: '19.00', r: '97.29', m: '89.28' }
Data Saved : { t: '21.00', h: '19.00', r: '97.53', m: '89.28' }
Data Saved : { t: '21.00', h: '19.00', r: '97.75', m: '89.33' }
Data Saved : { t: '21.00', h: '19.00', r: '97.92', m: '89.36' }
Data Saved : { t: '21.00', h: '19.00', r: '98.07', m: '89.38' }
Data Saved : { t: '21.00', h: '19.00', r: '98.22', m: '89.43' }
Data Saved : { t: '21.00', h: '19.00', r: '98.34', m: '89.48' }
Data Saved : { t: '21.00', h: '19.00', r: '98.44', m: '89.55' }
Data Saved : { t: '21.00', h: '19.00', r: '98.51', m: '89.53' }
Data Saved : { t: '21.00', h: '19.00', r: '98.58', m: '89.55' }
Data Saved : { t: '21.00', h: '19.00', r: '98.66', m: '89.55' }
Data Saved : { t: '21.00', h: '19.00', r: '98.73', m: '89.58' }
Data Saved : { t: '21.00', h: '19.00', r: '98.78', m: '89.60' }
```

The data from the device is logged here.

In the next section, we are going to update the web app so it can represent the data from the API engine.

Setting up the web app

Now that we are done with the API engine, we are going to develop the interface needed to show the weather output from the Raspberry Pi 3.

Open `web-app/src/app/device/device.component.html` and update it, as shown here:

```html
<div class="container">
    <br>
    <div *ngIf="!device">
        <h3 class="text-center">Loading!</h3>
    </div>
    <div class="row" *ngIf="lastRecord">
        <div class="col-md-12">
            <div class="panel panel-info">
                <div class="panel-heading">
                    <h3 class="panel-title">
                        {{device.name}}
                    </h3>
                    <span class="pull-right btn-click">
                        <i class="fa fa-chevron-circle-up"></i>
                    </span>
                </div>
                <div class="clearfix"></div>
                <div class="table-responsive">
                    <table class="table table-striped">
                        <tr *ngIf="lastRecord">
                            <td>Temperature</td>
                            <td>{{lastRecord.data.t}}</td>
                        </tr>
                        <tr *ngIf="lastRecord">
                            <td>Humidity</td>
                            <td>{{lastRecord.data.h}} %</td>
                        </tr>
                        <tr *ngIf="lastRecord">
                            <td>Rain Level</td>
                            <td>{{lastRecord.data.r}} %</td>
                        </tr>
                        <tr *ngIf="lastRecord">
                            <td>Mositure Level</td>
                            <td>{{lastRecord.data.m}} %</td>
                        </tr>
                        <tr *ngIf="lastRecord">
                            <td>Received At</td>
                            <td>{{lastRecord.createdAt | date:
'medium'}}</td>
```

```
                    </tr>
                </table>
                <div class="col-md-6" *ngIf="tempHumdData.length > 0">
                    <canvas baseChart [datasets]="tempHumdData"
[labels]="lineChartLabels" [options]="lineChartOptions"
[legend]="lineChartLegend" [chartType]="lineChartType"></canvas>
                </div>

                <div class="col-md-6" *ngIf="rainMoisData.length > 0">
                    <canvas baseChart [datasets]="rainMoisData"
[labels]="lineChartLabels" [options]="lineChartOptions"
[legend]="lineChartLegend" [chartType]="lineChartType"></canvas>
                </div>
            </div>
        </div>
    </div>
</div>
```

In the preceding code, we have added four rows in a table that displays temperature, humidity, rain level, and moisture level. We have also set up the canvas to display the values in the chart.

Next is the class definition for DeviceComponent, present in web-app/src/app/device/device.component.ts. Update web-app/src/app/device/device.component.ts, as shown here:

```
import { Component, OnInit, OnDestroy } from '@angular/core';
import { DevicesService } from '../services/devices.service';
import { Params, ActivatedRoute } from '@angular/router';
import { SocketService } from '../services/socket.service';
import { DataService } from '../services/data.service';
import { NotificationsService } from 'angular2-notifications';

@Component({
    selector: 'app-device',
    templateUrl: './device.component.html',
    styleUrls: ['./device.component.css']
})
export class DeviceComponent implements OnInit, OnDestroy {
    device: any;
    data: Array<any>;
    toggleState: boolean = false;
    privatesubDevice: any;
    privatesubData: any;
    lastRecord: any;
```

```
// line chart config
publiclineChartOptions: any = {
      responsive: true,
      legend: {
            position: 'bottom',
      }, hover: {
            mode: 'label'
      }, scales: {
            xAxes: [{
                  display: true,
                  scaleLabel: {
                        display: true,
                        labelString: 'Time'
                  }
            }],
            yAxes: [{
                  display: true,
                  ticks: {
                        beginAtZero: true,
                        // steps: 10,
                        // stepValue: 5,
                        // max: 70
                  }
            }]
      },
      title: {
            display: true,
            text: 'Sensor Data vs. Time'
      }
};
publiclineChartLegend: boolean = true;
publiclineChartType: string = 'line';
publictempHumdData: Array<any> = [];
publicrainMoisData: Array<any> = [];
publiclineChartLabels: Array<any> = [];

constructor(private deviceService: DevicesService,
      privatesocketService: SocketService,
      privatedataService: DataService,
      private route: ActivatedRoute,
      privatenotificationsService: NotificationsService) { }

ngOnInit() {
      this.subDevice = this.route.params.subscribe((params) => {
            this.deviceService.getOne(params['id']).subscribe((response)
=> {
                  this.device = response.json();
                  this.getData();
```

```
                this.socketInit();
            });
        });
    }

    getData() {
        this.dataService.get(this.device.macAddress).subscribe((response)
=> {
            this.data = response.json();
            this.lastRecord = this.data[0]; // descending order data
            this.genChart();
        });
    }

    socketInit() {
        this.subData =
this.socketService.getData(this.device.macAddress).subscribe((data) => {
            if (this.data.length<= 0) return;
            this.data.splice(this.data.length - 1, 1); // remove the
last record
            this.data.push(data); // add the new one
            this.lastRecord = data;
            this.genChart();
        });
    }

    ngOnDestroy() {
        this.subDevice.unsubscribe();
        this.subData ? this.subData.unsubscribe() : '';
    }

    genChart() {
        let data = this.data;
        let _thArr: Array<any> = [];
        let _rmArr: Array<any> = [];
        let _lblArr: Array<any> = [];

        lettmpArr: Array<any> = [];
        lethumArr: Array<any> = [];
        letraiArr: Array<any> = [];
        letmoiArr: Array<any> = [];

        for (vari = 0; i<data.length; i++) {
            let _d = data[i];
            tmpArr.push(_d.data.t);
            humArr.push(_d.data.h);
            raiArr.push(_d.data.r);
            moiArr.push(_d.data.m);
```

```
                    _lblArr.push(this.formatDate(_d.createdAt));
        }

        // reverse data to show the latest on the right side
        tmpArr.reverse();
        humArr.reverse();
        raiArr.reverse();
        moiArr.reverse();
        _lblArr.reverse();

        _thArr = [
                {
                        data: tmpArr,
                        label: 'Temperature'
                },
                {
                        data: humArr,
                        label: 'Humidity %'
                }
        ]

        _rmArr = [
                {
                        data: raiArr,
                        label: 'Rain Levels'
                },
                {
                        data: moiArr,
                        label: 'Moisture Levels'
                }
        ]

        this.tempHumdData = _thArr;
        this.rainMoisData = _rmArr;

        this.lineChartLabels = _lblArr;
    }

    privateformatDate(originalTime) {
        var d = new Date(originalTime);
        vardatestring = d.getDate() + "-" + (d.getMonth() + 1) + "-" +
d.getFullYear() + " " +
                d.getHours() + ":" + d.getMinutes();
        returndatestring;
    }

}
```

In the preceding code, we have used the `ngOnInit` hook and have made a request to get the device data. Using `socketInit()`, along with the data, we are going to register for socket data events for the current device.

In `getData()`, we fetch the data from the server, extract the latest record, and set it to the `lastRecord` property. And finally, we call `genChart()` to draw a chart.

Now, we are done with the required changes. Save all the files and run the following:

```
ng server
```

If we navigate to `http://localhost:4200`, log in, and click on **VIEW DEVICE**, we should see the following:

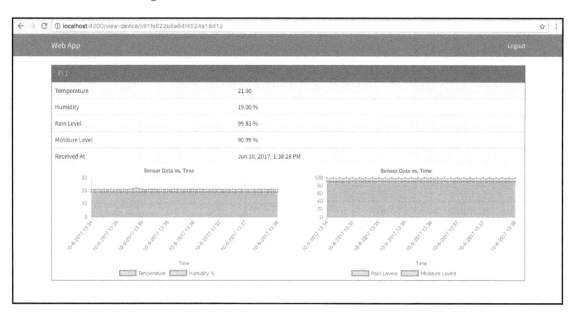

Whenever there is change in the data, we should see the UI update automatically.

In the next section, we are going to build the same app and show it inside the electron shell.

Setting up the desktop app

In the last section, we developed the template and interface for the web app. In this section, we are going to build the same thing and dump it inside the desktop app.

To get started, head back to the terminal/prompt of the web-app folder, and run the following:

```
ng build --env=prod
```

This will create a new folder inside the web-app folder named dist. The contents of the dist folder should consist of:

```
.
├── favicon.ico
├── index.html
├── inline.bundle.js
├── inline.bundle.js.map
├── main.bundle.js
├── main.bundle.js.map
├── polyfills.bundle.js
├── polyfills.bundle.js.map
├── scripts.bundle.js
├── scripts.bundle.js.map
├── styles.bundle.js
├── styles.bundle.js.map
├── vendor.bundle.js
└── vendor.bundle.js.map
```

All the code we have written is finally bundled into the preceding files. We will grab all the files (not the `dist` folder) present inside the `dist` folder and then paste them inside the `desktop-app/app` folder. The final structure of desktop-app after the preceding changes will be as follows:

```
├── app
│   ├── favicon.ico
│   ├── index.html
│   ├── inline.bundle.js
│   ├── inline.bundle.js.map
│   ├── main.bundle.js
│   ├── main.bundle.js.map
│   ├── polyfills.bundle.js
│   ├── polyfills.bundle.js.map
│   ├── scripts.bundle.js
│   ├── scripts.bundle.js.map
│   ├── styles.bundle.js
│   ├── styles.bundle.js.map
│   ├── vendor.bundle.js
│   └── vendor.bundle.js.map
├── freeport.js
├── index.css
├── index.html
├── index.js
├── license
```

```
├── package.json

├── readme.md

└── server.js
```

To test drive the process, run the following:

```
npm start
```

Navigate to the **VIEW DEVICE** page, and we should see the following:

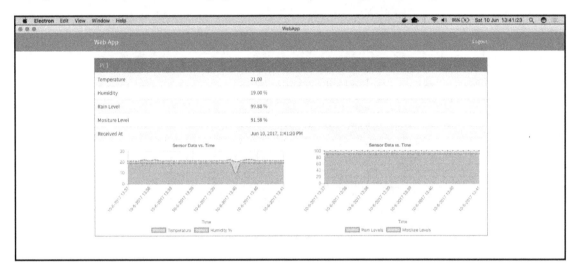

Whenever there is a change in the data, we should see the UI update automatically.

With this, we are done with the development of the desktop app. In the next section, we will update the mobile app.

Setting up the mobile app

In the last section, we saw how to build and run the desktop app for the smart weather station. In this section, we are going to update the template of the mobile app to show the weather station data.

Open `mobile-app/src/pages/view-device/view-device.html` and update it, as shown here:

```
<ion-header>
    <ion-navbar>
        <ion-title>Mobile App</ion-title>
    </ion-navbar>
</ion-header>
<ion-content padding>
    <div *ngIf="!lastRecord">
        <h3 class="text-center">Loading!</h3>
    </div>
    <div *ngIf="lastRecord">
        <ion-list>
            <ion-item>
                <ion-label>Name</ion-label>
                <ion-label>{{device.name}}</ion-label>
            </ion-item>
            <ion-item>
                <ion-label>Temperature</ion-label>
                <ion-label>{{lastRecord.data.t}}</ion-label>
            </ion-item>
            <ion-item>
                <ion-label>Humidity</ion-label>
                <ion-label>{{lastRecord.data.h}} %</ion-label>
            </ion-item>
            <ion-item>
                <ion-label>Rain Level</ion-label>
                <ion-label>{{lastRecord.data.r}} %</ion-label>
            </ion-item>
            <ion-item>
                <ion-label>Moisture Level</ion-label>
                <ion-label>{{lastRecord.data.m}} %</ion-label>
            </ion-item>
            <ion-item>
                <ion-label>Received At</ion-label>
                <ion-label>{{lastRecord.createdAt | date: 'medium'}}</ion-
label>
            </ion-item>
        </ion-list>
    </div>
</ion-content>
```

In the preceding code, we have created four items inside the list view to display the temperature, humidity, rain level, and moisture level. And the required logic for `ViewDevicePage` class would be present in `mobile-app/src/pages/view-device/view-device.ts`. Update `mobile-app/src/pages/view-device/view-device.ts`, as shown here:

```
import { Component } from '@angular/core';
import { IonicPage, NavController, NavParams } from 'ionic-angular';

import { DevicesService } from '../../services/device.service';
import { DataService } from '../../services/data.service';
import { ToastService } from '../../services/toast.service';
import { SocketService } from '../../services/socket.service';

@IonicPage()
@Component({
    selector: 'page-view-device',
    templateUrl: 'view-device.html',
})
export class ViewDevicePage {
    device: any;
    data: Array<any>;
    toggleState: boolean = false;
    privatesubData: any;
    lastRecord: any;


    constructor(private navCtrl: NavController,
            privatenavParams: NavParams,
            privatesocketService: SocketService,
            privatedeviceService: DevicesService,
            privatedataService: DataService,
            privatetoastService: ToastService) {
        this.device = navParams.get("device");
        console.log(this.device);
    }

    ionViewDidLoad() {
        this.deviceService.getOne(this.device._id).subscribe((response) =>
{
            this.device = response.json();
            this.getData();
            this.socketInit();
        });
    }

    getData() {
```

```
            this.dataService.get(this.device.macAddress).subscribe((response)
    => {
                this.data = response.json();
                this.lastRecord = this.data[0]; // descending order data
            });
        }

    socketInit() {
            this.subData =
    this.socketService.getData(this.device.macAddress).subscribe((data) => {
                if(this.data.length<= 0) return;
                this.data.splice(this.data.length - 1, 1); // remove the
    last record
                this.data.push(data); // add the new one
                this.lastRecord = data;
            });
        }

    ionViewDidUnload() {
    this.subData&&this.subData.unsubscribe&&this.subData.unsubscribe();
    //unsubscribe if subData is defined
        }
    }
```

In the preceding code, we are getting the latest data from the API engine using `getData()`. Then, using `socketInit()`, we are subscribing to the latest changes to the data.

 Check the IP address of the server on which the API engine is running. Update the same IP in your mobile app's `mobile-app/src/app/app.globals.ts` file. Otherwise, the mobile app cannot communicate with the API engine.

Now, save all the files and run the following:

ionic serve

Or, you can deploy the same to your device as well, by running the following:

ionic run android

Or

ionic run ios

Once the app is launched, and when we navigate to the **VIEW DEVICE** page, we should see the following on our screen:

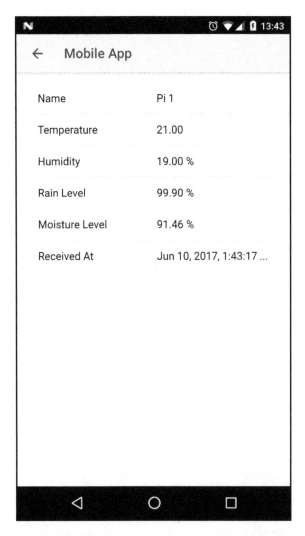

As we can see from the image, we are able to view the data updating in real time.

Summary

In this chapter, we used the knowledge we gained in chapters two and three and built a prototype of a smart weather station. We started by identifying the sensors needed to build the weather station. Next, we set them up on the Raspberry Pi 3. We wrote the code needed to interface with the sensors. Once this was done, we updated the API engine to read the data from the Raspberry Pi 3 on the new topic. Once the API engine received the data, we saved it in the database and then sent it to the web, desktop, and mobile apps over web-sockets. Finally, we updated the presentation templates on the web, desktop, and mobile apps; then, we displayed the data from the Raspberry Pi on the web, desktop, and mobile apps.

In `Chapter 5`, *Smart Agriculture and Voice AI*, we are going to work with voice artificial intelligence, using Alexa from Amazon and the smart weather station we built.

5

Smart Agriculture and Voice AI

In Chapter 4, *Smart Agriculture*, we have seen one of the mainstream areas in which IoT can create an impact; the agriculture sector. In this chapter, we are going to take that to a new level. Using a voice AI engine such as Amazon Alexa, we are going to talk to the smart weather station that we have built.

For example, a farmer can ask Alexa `Alexa, ask smarty app the moisture level in my farm, and Alexa would go *the moisture level in your farm is 20%. Consider watering now*. Then, the farmer would go, *Alexa, ask smarty app to turn on my motor* and Alexa would turn it on. Fascinating, isn't it?

Generally, voice AI based IoT is more common in the concepts of smart home and smart office. I wanted to implement it with smart agriculture.

In this chapter, we are going to work on the following:

- Understand Amazon Alexa
- Build an IoT.js controlled water motor
- Understand AWS lambda
- Develop a skillset for Amazon Alexa
- Test the weather station as well as the water motor

Voice AI

There was a time when turning something on/off using a smart phone was exciting. Times have changed and things have evolved quite a bit since in the space of voice AI. A lot of people use their voice to do a lot of things, right from making notes, building their grocery lists, to searching the internet. We no longer use hands for mundane activities.

"Look Ma, No hands!"

What's next? Think of it and it happens? I would love to be alive to see that, as I could do things at the speed of thought.

If you are new to the world of Voice AI, you can start looking up Amazon Alexa, Google Now/Google Assistant, Apple Siri, or Windows Cortana to see what I am talking about. Since we are going to work with Amazon Alexa in this chapter, we will explore only that.

Amazon recently launched a couple of devices named Amazon Echo and Amazon Echo Dot (recently made available in India too), which are smart speakers, enabled by Alexa, Amazon's voice AI software. If you want to experience Alexa for yourself, without buying buying echo products, download the reverb app for Android:
`https://play.google.com/store/apps/details?id=agency.rain.android.alexa&hl=en`
or iOS:
`https://itunes.apple.com/us/app/reverb-for-amazon-alexa/id1144695621?mt=8` and launch the app.

You should see an interface with a microphone icon. Press and hold the microphone and you should see the text **Listening...** on the top, as shown in the following screenshot:

Now say, *Alexa, tell me a joke* and get entertained by Alexa!

Test drive

To test what we are going to build, press the microphone icon in the reverb app and say, *Alexa, ask smarty app for the weather report* and you should hear the latest data that is persisted in the database for the smart weather station. And then you can say, *Alexa, ask smarty app to turn on the motor*, or *Alexa, ask smarty app to turn off the motor;* if my device is online, it will turn it off.

Along with smart weather station, we are going to build a smart socket, which can be connected to a motor in a farm. And using Alexa, we are going to turn on/off the motor.

Now, if you have an Amazon echo or echo dot, you can test the skill we are going to build. Or, you can do the same using the reverb app. You can also use `https://reverb.ai/` or `https://echosim.io/` for the same.

 Till your Alexa skill is published, it will be only accessible on devices that are linked with your Amazon account only. If you have enabled beta testing, then you can allow multiple people to access this skill on their Amazon account linked Alexa powered devices.

If you are facing issues to explore the demo, check out this video recording: `/videos/chapter5/alexa_smarty_app_demo.mov`

So, let's get started!

Building a smart socket

In this section, we are going to build a smart socket. The setup is going to be quite similar to what we had in `Chapter 4`, *Smart Agriculture*. Create a new folder named `chapter5` and copy the contents of the `chapter4` folder into it. The `chapter4` folder has the code for the smart weather station, and now, we are going to add the required code for smart socket.

The smart socket is a simple electrical socket that can be controlled over the internet. That is, turn on the socket and turn off the socket. We are going to use a **mechanical relay** to achieve this.

We are going to start off by setting up the relay with the other sensors on the Raspberry Pi. I am going to use one Raspberry Pi to demonstrate the smart weather station as well as the smart socket. You can use two Raspberry Pis as well for this.

We are going to add the appropriate MQTT client code to the API engine; next, update the web, desktop, and mobile app to have a toggle switch to turn on/off the relay.

We are going to create a new topic named `socket` on, which we would send either 1 or 0 to turn on/off the relay, thus turning the load on the other end of the relay on/off.

Do remember that we are exploring the various solutions that can be built with IoT and we are not building the final product itself.

Setting up relay with Raspberry Pi

As of now, Raspberry Pi has the smart weather station sensors attached to it. Now, we are going to add a relay to the setup.

A relay is an electrical switch that is driven by an electronic signal. That is, triggering the relay with logic high 1 will turn on the relay and logic low 0 will turn off the relay.

Some relays work the other way around, depending on the component. To know more about types of relay and how they work, refer to, `https://www.phidgets.com/docs/Mechanical_Relay_Primer`.

You can purchase a simple 5V driven relay from Amazon: (`https://www.amazon.com/DAOKI%C2%AE-Arduino-Indicator-Channel-Official/dp/B00XT0OSUQ/ref=sr_1_3`).

 Relays deal with AC current, and in our examples, we are not going to connect any AC power supply to the relay. We are going to power it using a 5V DC supply from Raspberry Pi and using the LED indicator on the relay identify if the relay has been turned on or off. In case you want to connect it to an actual power supply, please take adequate precaution before doing so. The results might be shocking if proper care is not taken.

Along with the weather station, we are going to connect the relay as well to the Raspberry Pi 3. Connect the relay, as shown in the following figure.

Connection of Raspberry Pi with the smart weather station:

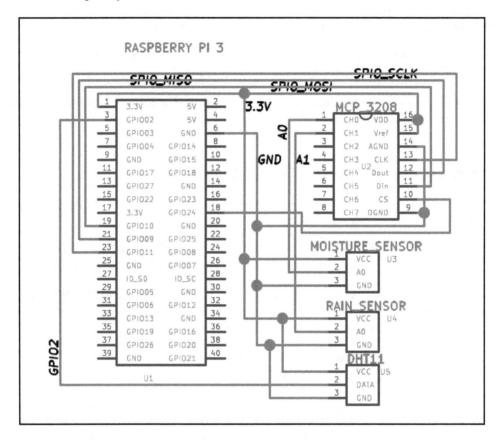

Connection of Raspberry Pi with a `relay` (module):

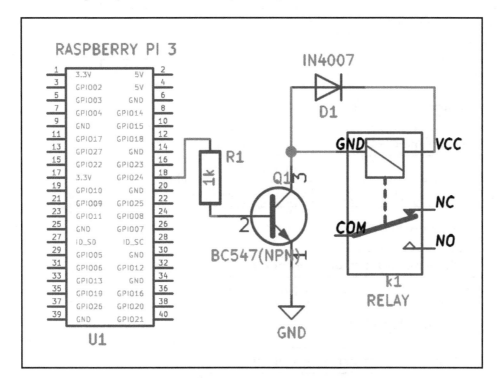

 If you purchased a standalone relay, you need to set up the circuit, as shown previously. And, if you have purchased the relay module, you need to connect pin 18/GPIO24 to the trigger pin, after powering the relay.

To reiterate the previous connection, please see the tables shown, as follows:

- Raspberry Pi and MCP3208:

Raspberry Pi number - Pin name	MCP 3208 pin number - Pin name
1 - 3.3V	16 - VDD
1 - 3.3V	15 - AREF
6 - GND	14 - AGND
23 - GPIO11, SPI0_SCLK	13 - CLK

21 - GPIO09, SPI0_MISO	12 - DOUT
19 - GPIO10, SPI0_MOSI	11 - DIN
24 - GPIO08, CEO	10 - CS
6 - GND	9 - DGND

- Moisture sensor and MCP3208:

MCP 3208 pin number - Pin name	Sensor pin
1 - A0	Rain sensor - A0
1 - A1	Moisture sensor - A0

- Raspberry Pi and DHT11:

Raspberry Pi number - Pin name	Sensor pin
3 - GPIO2	DHT11 - data

- Raspberry Pi and relay:

Raspberry Pi number - Pin name	Sensor pin
12 - GPIO18	Relay - trigger pin

All grounds and all 3.3V pins are connected to a common point. All the relay needs is a 5V power supply from the Raspberry Pi, which is pin 2.

Once we have connected the sensors as shown previously, we will write the required code needed to interface with the sensors.

Head towards the `pi-client` folder inside `Raspberry Pi 3`, open `pi-client/index.js`, and update it as follows:

```
var config = require('./config.js');
var mqtt = require('mqtt');
var GetMac = require('getmac');
var async = require('async');
var rpiDhtSensor = require('rpi-dht-sensor');
var McpAdc = require('mcp-adc');
var adc = new McpAdc.Mcp3208();
var rpio = require('rpio');
```

```
// Set pin 12 as output pin and to low
rpio.open(12, rpio.OUTPUT, rpio.LOW);

var dht11 = new rpiDhtSensor.DHT11(2);
var temp = 0,
    prevTemp = 0;
var humd = 0,
    prevHumd = 0;
var macAddress;
var state = 0;

var mositureVal = 0,
    prevMositureVal = 0;
var rainVal = 0,
    prevRainVal = 0;

var client = mqtt.connect({
    port: config.mqtt.port,
    protocol: 'mqtts',
    host: config.mqtt.host,
    clientId: config.mqtt.clientId,
    reconnectPeriod: 1000,
    username: config.mqtt.clientId,
    password: config.mqtt.clientId,
    keepalive: 300,
    rejectUnauthorized: false
});

client.on('connect', function() {
    client.subscribe('rpi');
    client.subscribe('socket');
    GetMac.getMac(function(err, mac) {
        if (err) throw err;
        macAddress = mac;
        client.publish('api-engine', mac);
    });
});

client.on('message', function(topic, message) {
    message = message.toString();
    if (topic === 'rpi') {
        console.log('API Engine Response >> ', message);
    } else if (topic === 'socket') {
        state = parseInt(message)
        console.log('Turning Relay', !state ? 'On' : 'Off');
        // Relays are almost always active low
        //console.log(!state ? rpio.HIGH : rpio.LOW);
        // If we get a 1 we turn on the relay, else off
```

```
            rpio.write(12, !state ? rpio.HIGH : rpio.LOW);
        } else {
            console.log('Unknown topic', topic);
        }
});

// infinite loop, with 3 seconds delay
setInterval(function() {
    readSensorValues(function(results) {
        console.log('Temperature: ' + temp + 'C, ' + 'humidity: ' + humd +
'%, ' + ' Rain level (%):' + rainVal + ', ' + 'mositureVal (%): ' +
mositureVal);
        // if the temperature and humidity values change
        // then only publish the values
        if (temp !== prevTemp || humd !== prevHumd || mositureVal !==
prevMositureVal || rainVal != prevRainVal) {
            var data2Send = {
                data: {
                    t: temp,
                    h: humd,
                    r: rainVal,
                    m: mositureVal,
                    s: state
                },
                macAddress: macAddress
            };
            // console.log('Data Published');
            client.publish('weather-status', JSON.stringify(data2Send));
            // reset prev values to current
            // for next loop
            prevTemp = temp;
            prevHumd = humd;
            prevMositureVal = mositureVal;
            prevRainVal = rainVal;
        }
    });
}, 3000); // every three second


function readSensorValues(CB) {
    async.parallel({
        dht11Values: function(callback) {
            var readout = dht11.read();
            // update global variable
            temp = readout.temperature.toFixed(2);
            humd = readout.humidity.toFixed(2);
            callback(null, { temp: temp, humidity: humd });
        },
```

```
        rainLevel: function(callback) {
            // we are going to connect rain sensor
            // on channel 0, hence 0 is the first arg below
            adc.readRawValue(0, function(value) {
                // update global variable
                rainVal = value;
                rainVal = (100 - parseFloat((rainVal / 4096) *
100)).toFixed(2);
                callback(null, { rain: rainVal });
            });
        },
        moistureLevel: function(callback) {
            // we are going to connect mositure sensor
            // on channel 1, hence 1 is the first arg below
            adc.readRawValue(1, function(value) {
                // update global variable
                mositureVal = value;
                mositureVal = (100 - parseFloat((mositureVal / 4096) *
100)).toFixed(2);
                callback(null, { moisture: mositureVal });
            });
        }
    }, function done(err, results) {
        if (err) {
            throw err;
        }
        // console.log(results);
        if (CB) CB(results);
    });
}
```

To the `Weather Station` code, we have added the `rpio` module and using the `rpio.open()`, we have made pin 12 as an output pin. We are also listening to the topic named socket. And, when we get a response from the broker on this topic, we set pin 12 to high or low based on the data.

Now, we will install the `rpio` module inside the Raspberry Pi `pi-client` folder, and run the following command:

npm install rpio -save

Save all, the files. Now, we will start the Mosca broker from our desktop/machine:

mosca -c index.js -v | pino

Once you have started Mosca server, do check the IP address of the server on which Mosca is running. Update the same IP in your Raspberry Pi `config.js` file or else Raspberry Pi cannot post data to the broker.

Once Mosca has started successfully and we have validated the IP on the Raspberry Pi, run:

sudo node index.js

This will start the server and keep sending the weather information to the broker.

In the next section, we are going to write the required logic needed for the API engine to process the relay.

Managing relay in an API engine

Now that the relay is connected to the Raspberry Pi, we will write the logic that will send the on/off command to the socket topic. Open `api-engine/server/mqtt/index.js` and update it, as follows:

```
var Data = require('../api/data/data.model');
var mqtt = require('mqtt');
var config = require('../config/environment');

var client = mqtt.connect({
    port: config.mqtt.port,
    protocol: 'mqtts',
    host: config.mqtt.host,
    clientId: config.mqtt.clientId,
    reconnectPeriod: 1000,
    username: config.mqtt.clientId,
    password: config.mqtt.clientId,
    keepalive: 300,
    rejectUnauthorized: false
});

client.on('connect', function() {
    console.log('Connected to Mosca at ' + config.mqtt.host + ' on port ' +
config.mqtt.port);
    client.subscribe('api-engine');
    client.subscribe('weather-status');
});

client.on('message', function(topic, message) {
    // message is Buffer
```

```
        // console.log('Topic >> ', topic);
        // console.log('Message >> ', message.toString());
        if (topic === 'api-engine') {
            var macAddress = message.toString();
            console.log('Mac Address >> ', macAddress);
            client.publish('rpi', 'Got Mac Address: ' + macAddress);
        } else if (topic === 'weather-status') {
            var data = JSON.parse(message.toString());
            // create a new data record for the device
            Data.create(data, function(err, data) {
                if (err) return console.error(err);
                // if the record has been saved successfully,
                // websockets will trigger a message to the web-app
                console.log('Data Saved :', data.data);
            });
        } else {
            console.log('Unknown topic', topic);
        }
});

exports.sendSocketData = function(data) {
    console.log('Sending Data', data);
    client.publish('socket', JSON.stringify(data));
}
```

We have added a method named `sendSocketData` and exported it. We are going to call this method in the `api-engine/server/api/data/data.controller.js`create method, as follows:

```
exports.create = function(req, res, next) {
    var data = req.body;
    data.createdBy = req.user._id;
    Data.create(data, function(err, _data) {
        if (err) return res.status(500).send(err);
        if (data.topic === 'socket') {
            require('../../mqtt/index.js').sendSocketData(_data.data.s); //
send relay value
        }
        return res.json(_data);
    });
};
```

Save all, the files and run:

npm start

You should get the following on your screen:

```
→ api-engine npm start

> api-engine@0.1.0 start /Users/arvindravulavaru/Arvind/Books/Advanced IoT with JS/code/chapter5/api-engine
> nodemon server/app.js

[nodemon] 1.10.0
[nodemon] to restart at any time, enter `rs`
[nodemon] watching: *.*
[nodemon] starting `node server/app.js`
Express server listening on 9000, in development mode
Connected to Mosca at 127.0.0.1 on port 8883
[Wv09_Q5Ij-KqLO-6AAAA] Connected on 127.0.0.1
[X3T9wA0vwXe7aNsYAAAB] Connected on 192.168.10.11
Mac Address >> b8:27:eb:39:92:0d
Data Saved : { t: '0.00', h: '0.00', r: '48.36', m: '69.65', s: 0 }
Data Saved : { t: '26.00', h: '26.00', r: '48.29', m: '69.63', s: 0 }
Data Saved : { t: '26.00', h: '27.00', r: '48.49', m: '69.65', s: 0 }
Data Saved : { t: '26.00', h: '26.00', r: '48.27', m: '69.63', s: 0 }
Data Saved : { t: '26.00', h: '26.00', r: '48.07', m: '69.60', s: 0 }
Data Saved : { t: '23.00', h: '18.00', r: '47.95', m: '69.60', s: 0 }
Data Saved : { t: '26.00', h: '26.00', r: '48.05', m: '69.65', s: 0 }
Data Saved : { t: '26.00', h: '26.00', r: '47.92', m: '69.60', s: 0 }
Data Saved : { t: '26.00', h: '26.00', r: '47.71', m: '69.60', s: 0 }
Data Saved : { t: '26.00', h: '26.00', r: '47.92', m: '69.58', s: 0 }
Data Saved : { t: '26.00', h: '27.00', r: '47.90', m: '69.58', s: 0 }
Data Saved : { t: '26.00', h: '26.00', r: '47.90', m: '69.58', s: 0 }
Data Saved : { t: '26.00', h: '26.00', r: '47.85', m: '69.58', s: 0 }
Data Saved : { t: '26.00', h: '27.00', r: '47.75', m: '69.58', s: 0 }
Data Saved : { t: '26.00', h: '26.00', r: '47.66', m: '69.56', s: 0 }
Data Saved : { t: '26.00', h: '26.00', r: '47.68', m: '69.36', s: 0 }
Data Saved : { t: '26.00', h: '26.00', r: '47.63', m: '69.53', s: 0 }
```

Do note, the last value in the data string printed in the console; s, we are sending the status of the relay as well to display in the UI, if the relay is on/off.

With this, we are done with the code needed to develop the API engine. In the next section, we are going to work on the web app.

Updating the web app template

In this section, we are going to update the web app template to have a toggle button, quite similar to what we had in Chapter 2, *IoTFW.js - I*, and Chapter 3, *IoTFW.js - II*. Using the toggle button, we are going to turn on/off the relay manually. In the later sections, we are going to automate them.

Open, web-app/src/app/device/device.component.html and update it, as follows:

```
<div class="container">
    <br>
    <div *ngIf="!device">
```

```
            <h3 class="text-center">Loading!</h3>
        </div>
    <div class="row" *ngIf="lastRecord">
        <div class="col-md-12">
            <div class="panel panel-info">
                <div class="panel-heading">
                    <h3 class="panel-title">
                        {{device.name}}
                    </h3>
                    <span class="pull-right btn-click">
                        <i class="fa fa-chevron-circle-up"></i>
                    </span>
                </div>
                <div class="clearfix"></div>
                <div class="table-responsive">
                    <table class="table table-striped">
                        <tr>
                            <td>Toggle Socket</td>
                            <td>
                                <ui-switch [(ngModel)]="toggleState"
(change)="toggleChange($event)"></ui-switch>
                            </td>
                        </tr>
                        <tr *ngIf="lastRecord">
                            <td>Temperature</td>
                            <td>{{lastRecord.data.t}}</td>
                        </tr>
                        <tr *ngIf="lastRecord">
                            <td>Humidity</td>
                            <td>{{lastRecord.data.h}} %</td>
                        </tr>
                        <tr *ngIf="lastRecord">
                            <td>Rain Level</td>
                            <td>{{lastRecord.data.r}} %</td>
                        </tr>
                        <tr *ngIf="lastRecord">
                            <td>Mositure Level</td>
                            <td>{{lastRecord.data.m}} %</td>
                        </tr>
                        <tr *ngIf="lastRecord">
                            <td>Received At</td>
                            <td>{{lastRecord.createdAt | date:
'medium'}}</td>
                        </tr>
                    </table>
                    <div class="col-md-6" *ngIf="tempHumdData.length > 0">
                        <canvas baseChart [datasets]="tempHumdData"
[labels]="lineChartLabels" [options]="lineChartOptions"
```

```
[legend]="lineChartLegend" [chartType]="lineChartType"></canvas>
                    </div>
                    <div class="col-md-6" *ngIf="rainMoisData.length > 0">
                        <canvas baseChart [datasets]="rainMoisData"
[labels]="lineChartLabels" [options]="lineChartOptions"
[legend]="lineChartLegend" [chartType]="lineChartType"></canvas>
                    </div>
                </div>
            </div>
        </div>
    </div>
</div>
```

All we have done is added a new row that shows a toggle button, and using this, we turn on/off the socket. Next, the required logic to manage the toggle button, open `web-app/src/app/device/device.component.ts` and update it, as follows:

```
import { Component, OnInit, OnDestroy } from '@angular/core';
import { DevicesService } from '../services/devices.service';
import { Params, ActivatedRoute } from '@angular/router';
import { SocketService } from '../services/socket.service';
import { DataService } from '../services/data.service';
import { NotificationsService } from 'angular2-notifications';

@Component({
    selector: 'app-device',
    templateUrl: './device.component.html',
    styleUrls: ['./device.component.css']
})
export class DeviceComponent implements OnInit, OnDestroy {
    device: any;
    data: Array<any>;
    toggleState: boolean = false;
    private subDevice: any;
    private subData: any;
    lastRecord: any;

    // line chart config
    public lineChartOptions: any = {
        responsive: true,
        legend: {
            position: 'bottom',
        }, hover: {
            mode: 'label'
        }, scales: {
            xAxes: [{
                display: true,
```

```
                            scaleLabel: {
                                display: true,
                                labelString: 'Time'
                            }
                    }],
                    yAxes: [{
                            display: true,
                            ticks: {
                                    beginAtZero: true,
                                    // steps: 10,
                                    // stepValue: 5,
                                    // max: 70
                            }
                    }]
            },
            title: {
                    display: true,
                    text: 'Sensor Data vs. Time'
            }
    };
    public lineChartLegend: boolean = true;
    public lineChartType: string = 'line';
    public tempHumdData: Array<any> = [];
    public rainMoisData: Array<any> = [];
    public lineChartLabels: Array<any> = [];

    constructor(private deviceService: DevicesService,
        private socketService: SocketService,
        private dataService: DataService,
        private route: ActivatedRoute,
        private notificationsService: NotificationsService) { }

    ngOnInit() {
        this.subDevice = this.route.params.subscribe((params) => {
                this.deviceService.getOne(params['id']).subscribe((response)
=> {
                        this.device = response.json();
                        this.getData();
                        this.socketInit();
                });
        });
    }

    getData() {
        this.dataService.get(this.device.macAddress).subscribe((response)
=> {
                this.data = response.json();
                this.lastRecord = this.data[0]; // descending order data
```

```
                this.toggleState = this.lastRecord.data.s;
                this.genChart();
        });
    }

    socketInit() {
            this.subData =
this.socketService.getData(this.device.macAddress).subscribe((data) => {
                if (this.data.length <= 0) return;
                this.data.splice(this.data.length - 1, 1); // remove the
last record
                this.data.push(data); // add the new one
                this.lastRecord = data;
                this.toggleState = this.lastRecord.data.s;
                this.genChart();
        });
    }

    toggleChange(state) {
            let data = {
                macAddress: this.device.macAddress,
                data: {
                        t: this.lastRecord.data.t,
                        h: this.lastRecord.data.h,
                        m: this.lastRecord.data.m,
                        r: this.lastRecord.data.r,
                        s: state ? 1 : 0
                },
                topic: 'socket'
            }

            this.dataService.create(data).subscribe((resp) => {
                if (resp.json()._id) {
                        this.notificationsService.success('Device Notified!');
                }
            }, (err) => {
                console.log(err);
                this.notificationsService.error('Device Notification Failed.
Check console for the error!');
            })
    }

    ngOnDestroy() {
            this.subDevice.unsubscribe();
            this.subData ? this.subData.unsubscribe() : '';
    }

    genChart() {
```

```
let data = this.data;
let _thArr: Array<any> = [];
let _rmArr: Array<any> = [];
let _lblArr: Array<any> = [];

let tmpArr: Array<any> = [];
let humArr: Array<any> = [];
let raiArr: Array<any> = [];
let moiArr: Array<any> = [];

for (var i = 0; i < data.length; i++) {
    let _d = data[i];
    tmpArr.push(_d.data.t);
    humArr.push(_d.data.h);
    raiArr.push(_d.data.r);
    moiArr.push(_d.data.m);
    _lblArr.push(this.formatDate(_d.createdAt));
}

// reverse data to show the latest on the right side
tmpArr.reverse();
humArr.reverse();
raiArr.reverse();
moiArr.reverse();
_lblArr.reverse();

_thArr = [
    {
        data: tmpArr,
        label: 'Temperature'
    },
    {
        data: humArr,
        label: 'Humidity %'
    }
]

_rmArr = [
    {
        data: raiArr,
        label: 'Rain Levels'
    },
    {
        data: moiArr,
        label: 'Moisture Levels'
    }
]
```

```
            this.tempHumdData = _thArr;
            this.rainMoisData = _rmArr;

            this.lineChartLabels = _lblArr;
    }

    private formatDate(originalTime) {
            var d = new Date(originalTime);
            var datestring = d.getDate() + "-" + (d.getMonth() + 1) + "-" +
    d.getFullYear() + " " +
                    d.getHours() + ":" + d.getMinutes();
            return datestring;
    }

}
```

All we have done here is manage the toggle button state. Save all the files and run the following:

ng serve

Navigate to `http://localhost:4200` and then navigate to the device page. Now, using the toggle button on the page, we can turn the relay on/off, as shown in the following screenshot:

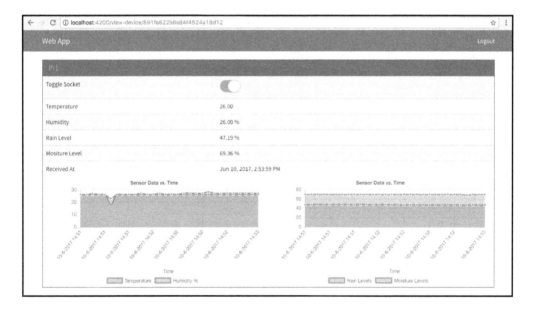

If everything is set up correctly, you should see the relay LED turn on/off on the relay, as shown in the following photograph:

Wires! Duh!

With this, we are done with the web app. In the next section, we are going to build the same web app and deploy it inside our desktop app.

Updating the desktop app

Now that the web app is done, we are going to build the same and deploy it inside our desktop app.

To get started, head back to the terminal/prompt of the web-app folder and run:

```
ng build --env=prod
```

This will create a new folder inside the `web-app` folder named `dist`. The contents of the `dist` folder should be on the lines of:

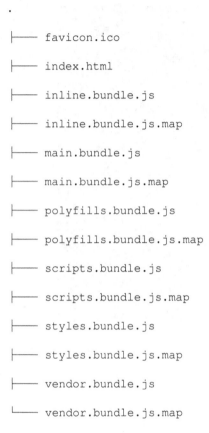

```
.
├── favicon.ico
├── index.html
├── inline.bundle.js
├── inline.bundle.js.map
├── main.bundle.js
├── main.bundle.js.map
├── polyfills.bundle.js
├── polyfills.bundle.js.map
├── scripts.bundle.js
├── scripts.bundle.js.map
├── styles.bundle.js
├── styles.bundle.js.map
├── vendor.bundle.js
└── vendor.bundle.js.map
```

All, the code we have written is finally bundled into the preceding files. We will grab all of the files (not the `dist` folder) present inside the `dist` folder and then paste it inside the `desktop-app/app` folder. The final structure of the `desktop-app` after the previous changes will be as follows:

```
.
├── app
│   ├── favicon.ico
│   ├── index.html
│   ├── inline.bundle.js
```

```
|   ├── inline.bundle.js.map
|   ├── main.bundle.js
|   ├── main.bundle.js.map
|   ├── polyfills.bundle.js
|   ├── polyfills.bundle.js.map
|   ├── scripts.bundle.js
|   ├── scripts.bundle.js.map
|   ├── styles.bundle.js
|   ├── styles.bundle.js.map
|   ├── vendor.bundle.js
|   └── vendor.bundle.js.map
├── freeport.js
├── index.css
├── index.html
├── index.js
├── license
├── package.json
├── readme.md
└── server.js
```

To test drive, run the following command:

```
npm start
```

Then, when we navigate to the **VIEW DEVICE** page, we should see the following:

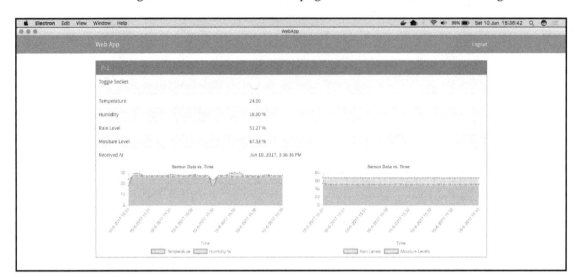

Using the toggle button, we should be able to turn the relay on/off.

With this, we are done with the development of the desktop app. In the next section, we will update the mobile app.

Updating the mobile app template

In the last section, we have updated the desktop app. In this section, we are going to update the mobile app template with the toggle switch component. So, using this toggle switch, we can turn the smart socket on/off.

First, we are going to update the view-device template. Update `mobile-app/src/pages/view-device/view-device.html`, as follows:

```
<ion-header>
    <ion-navbar>
        <ion-title>Mobile App</ion-title>
    </ion-navbar>
</ion-header>
<ion-content padding>
    <div *ngIf="!lastRecord">
        <h3 class="text-center">Loading!</h3>
    </div>
    <div *ngIf="lastRecord">
```

```
            <ion-list>
                <ion-item>
                    <ion-label>Name</ion-label>
                    <ion-label>{{device.name}}</ion-label>
                </ion-item>
                <ion-item>
                    <ion-label>Toggle LED</ion-label>
                    <ion-toggle [(ngModel)]="toggleState"
(click)="toggleChange($event)"></ion-toggle>
                </ion-item>
                <ion-item>
                    <ion-label>Temperature</ion-label>
                    <ion-label>{{lastRecord.data.t}}</ion-label>
                </ion-item>
                <ion-item>
                    <ion-label>Humidity</ion-label>
                    <ion-label>{{lastRecord.data.h}} %</ion-label>
                </ion-item>
                <ion-item>
                    <ion-label>Rain Level</ion-label>
                    <ion-label>{{lastRecord.data.r}} %</ion-label>
                </ion-item>
                <ion-item>
                    <ion-label>Moisture Level</ion-label>
                    <ion-label>{{lastRecord.data.m}} %</ion-label>
                </ion-item>
                <ion-item>
                    <ion-label>Received At</ion-label>
                    <ion-label>{{lastRecord.createdAt | date: 'medium'}}</ion-
label>
                </ion-item>
            </ion-list>
        </div>
</ion-content>
```

Next, we are going to add the required logic to manage the toggle button. Update `mobile-app/src/pages/view-device/view-device.ts`, as follows:

```
import { Component } from '@angular/core';
import { IonicPage, NavController, NavParams } from 'ionic-angular';

import { DevicesService } from '../../services/device.service';
import { DataService } from '../../services/data.service';
import { ToastService } from '../../services/toast.service';
import { SocketService } from '../../services/socket.service';

@IonicPage()
```

```
@Component({
    selector: 'page-view-device',
    templateUrl: 'view-device.html',
})
export class ViewDevicePage {
    device: any;
    data: Array<any>;
    toggleState: boolean = false;
    private subData: any;
    lastRecord: any;


    constructor(private navCtrl: NavController,
        private navParams: NavParams,
        private socketService: SocketService,
        private deviceService: DevicesService,
        private dataService: DataService,
        private toastService: ToastService) {
        this.device = navParams.get("device");
        console.log(this.device);
    }

    ionViewDidLoad() {
        this.deviceService.getOne(this.device._id).subscribe((response) =>
{
            this.device = response.json();
            this.getData();
            this.socketInit();
        });
    }

    getData() {
        this.dataService.get(this.device.macAddress).subscribe((response)
=> {
            this.data = response.json();
            this.lastRecord = this.data[0]; // descending order data
            if (this.lastRecord) {
                this.toggleState = this.lastRecord.data.s;
            }
        });
    }
    socketInit() {
        this.subData =
this.socketService.getData(this.device.macAddress).subscribe((data) => {
            if (this.data.length <= 0) return;
            this.data.splice(this.data.length - 1, 1); // remove the
last record
            this.data.push(data); // add the new one
```

```
                    this.lastRecord = data;
            });
    }

    toggleChange(state) {
        let data = {
                macAddress: this.device.macAddress,
                data: {
                        t: this.lastRecord.data.t,
                        h: this.lastRecord.data.h,
                        m: this.lastRecord.data.m,
                        r: this.lastRecord.data.r,
                        s: !state
                },
                topic: 'socket'
        }

        console.log(data);

        this.dataService.create(data).subscribe((resp) => {
                if (resp.json()._id) {
                        this.toastService.toggleToast('Device Notified!');
                }
        }, (err) => {
                console.log(err);
                this.toastService.toggleToast('Device Notification Failed.
Check console for the error!');
        })
    }

    ionViewDidUnload() {
        this.subData && this.subData.unsubscribe &&
this.subData.unsubscribe(); //unsubscribe if subData is defined
    }
}
```

Here, we have added the required logic to manage the toggle button. Save all, the files and run:

```
ionic serve
```

Or, you can deploy the same to your device as well, by running:

```
ionic run android
```

Or:

```
ionic run ios
```

Once the app is launched, and when we navigate to **VIEW DEVICE** page, we should see the following:

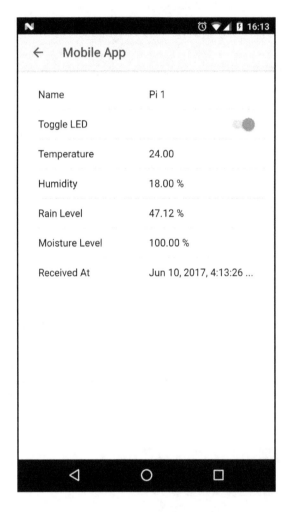

We should be able to control the socket using the toggle button on the mobile app.

With this, we are done with the set up of smart motor.

In the next section, we are going to build a new skill for Amazon Alexa.

Developing Alexa skill

In the last section, we have seen how to build a smart socket and integrate it with our existing smart weather station. In this section, we are going to build a new skill for interfacing our smart devices with Amazon Alexa.

We are going to create a new skill named smarty app and then add two voice models to it:

- To get the latest weather status
- To turn on/off the socket

If you are new to Alexa and its skill development, I would recommend watching the following series before you continue: Developing Alexa skills:
`https://www.youtube.com/playlist?list=PL2KJmkHeYQTO6ci5KF08mvHYd AZu2jgkJ`

To give a quick overview of our skill creation, we are going to follow these steps:

1. Log in to the Amazon developer portal and create and set up a new skill
2. Train the voice model
3. Write the required business logic in AWS lambda service
4. Deploy and test the setup

So, let's get started.

Creating skill

The first thing we are going to do is log in to `https://developer.amazon.com`. Once we are logged in, click on **Alexa** on the top section of the page. You should land on a page that should look as follows:

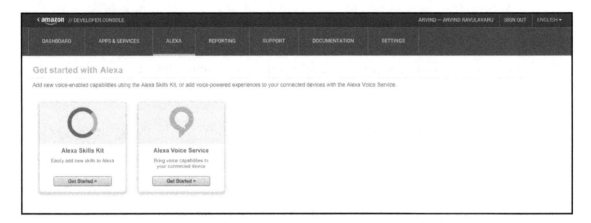

Click on **Get Started >** below **Alexa Skills Kit** and you should be redirected to a page where you can view your existing skill sets or create a new one. Click on the **golden** button on the top right-hand corner named **Add a new skill**.

You should be redirected to a page, as follows:

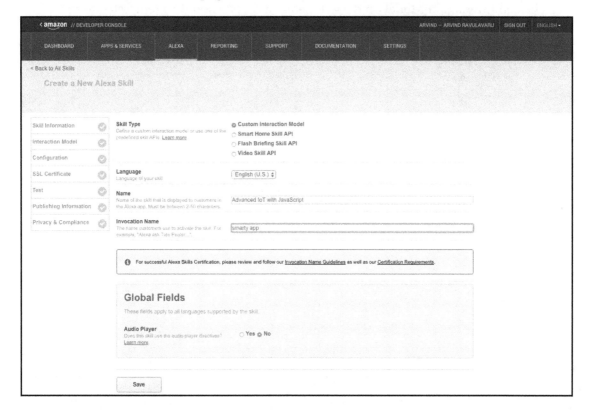

I have given the preceding information. You can configure it as you please. Click **Save** and then click on **Interaction Model** on the left menu, and you should be redirected to the **Interactive Model settings**, as follows:

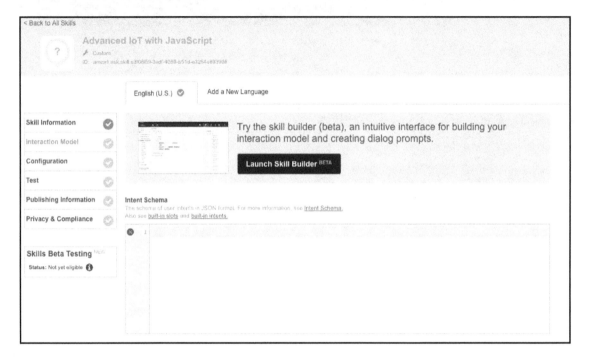

We are going to use the skill builder, which is still in beta at the time of writing. Skill builder is an easy interface to train our voice model.

Click on the **Launch Skill Builder** button.

Training the voice model

Once we are inside the skill builder, we are going to start training the models. In our application, we are going to have two intents:

- WeatherStatusIntent: To get the values of all four sensors
- ControlMotorIntent: To turn the motor on/off

Apart from this, you can also add other intents based on your requirements. You can add a moisture sensor only intent to get the values of moisture sensor only or rain sensor intent for only rain sensor values.

Now, we will go ahead and set up these intents and create slots.

Once you are inside the skill builder, you should see something similar to the following:

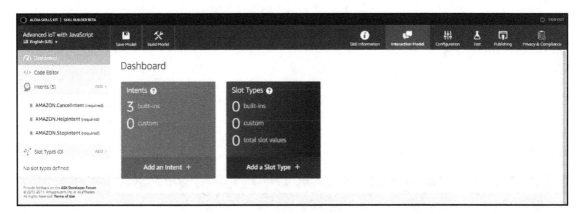

Now, using **Add +** next to the intents on the left-hand side, create a new custom intent and name it `WeatherStatusIntent`, as follows:

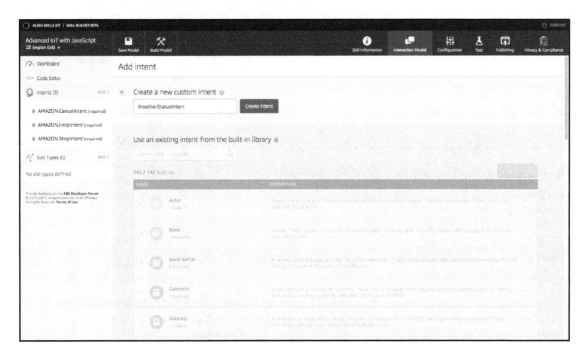

Now, we are going to train the voice model. Once the intent has been created, click on the intent name on the left menu. Now, we should see a section named **Sample Utterances**. We are going to feed the sample utterances of how the user is going to invoke our service.

To keep things simple, I have added only three samples:

Alexa, ask smarty app:

- The weather report
- The weather status
- The field conditions

You can see this in the following screenshot:

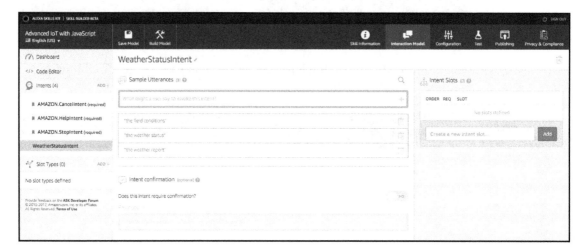

Next, we are going to create another intent named `ControlMotorIntent` using the same process. Click on **ControlMotorIntent** on the left-hand side menu and we should see the sample utterances section.

For this intent, we are going to do something different; we are going to create something called **slots**. We are going to take the sample utterance that the user would utter and extract a piece of it as a variable.

For example, if the user says, *Alexa, ask smarty app to turn on the motor*, or *Alexa, ask smarty app to turn off the motor*, everything is the same except for turn on or turn off, so we want to convert these to variables and handle each instruction differently.

If the slot is turned on, we turn on the motor and if the slot is turned off, we are going to turn off the motor.

So, once you have entered the sample utterance such as **to turn on the motor**, select the text turn on, as shown in the following screenshot:

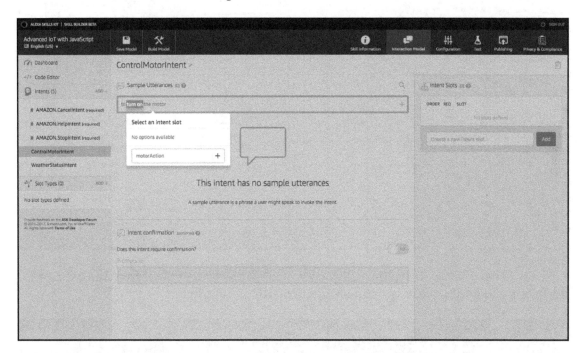

Once you have selected the text, enter a custom intent slot name **motorAction** and click on the *plus* icon.

We will have only one utterance for this intent. Next, we need to configure the **motorAction** intent slot.

On the right-hand side of the page, you should see the newly created intent slot. Check the checkbox under the **REQ** column. This means that this value is required for the intent to be called. Next, click on **Choose a slot type** below the slot name.

Here, we have to define a custom intent slot type. Add `motorActionIntentSlot`, as follows:

Next, we have to set up the values. Click on `motorActionIntentSlot` from the left-hand side menu and add two values; **turn on** and **turn off**, as follows:

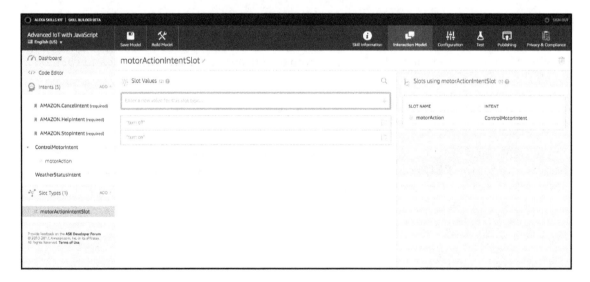

Once this is done, we need to set up the prompt that will be spoken when the user doesn't utter the two slot values we have defined. Click on **{motorAction}** under **ControlMotorIntent** and below **Dialog Model**, and enter a prompt such as `Do you want me to turn on or turn off the motor?`, as follows:

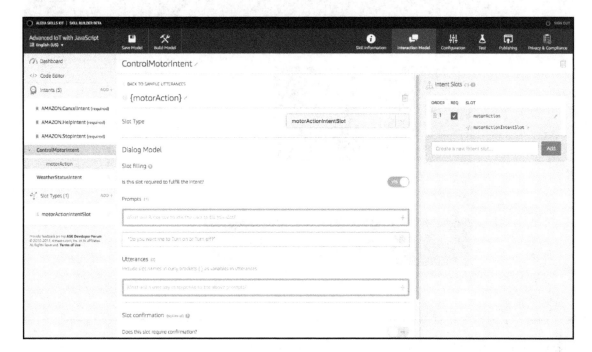

With this, we are done with defining our voice model.

Now, we need to ask the Alexa skill engine to build our voice model and add it to its skill engine. Using the **Save Model** button at the top of the page, save the model and then **Build Model**:

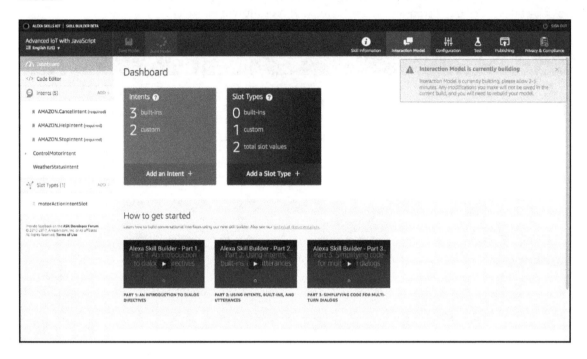

The build generally takes five minutes or less to complete.

ngrok the API engine

Before we go ahead and start working on the lambda service, we need to first expose our API engine to be available with a public URL, as in `http://iotfwjs.com/api`, so when the user asks the Alexa skill service a question or issues a command, the Alexa skill service can contact us via the lambda service.

So far, we have been using a local IP-based configuration to interact with the API engine, broker, web app, or Raspberry Pi. But, that doesn't work when we want, Alexa skill service to find us.

Hence, we are going to use a service named ngrok (https://ngrok.com/) to temporarily host our local code with a public URL that Amazon Alexa service can use to find us via lambda service.

To set up ngrok, please follow these steps:

1. Download the ngrok installer from here: https://ngrok.com/download for your OS, which is running the API engine
2. Unzip and copy the contents of the ngrok downloaded ZIP file at the root of the api-engine folder
3. Start Mosca from the root of the broker folder, by running the following command:

    ```
    mosca -c index.js -v | pino
    ```

4. Start the API engine from the root of api-engine folder, by running:

    ```
    npm start
    ```

5. Start tunneling with ngrok now. From the root of the api-engine folder, where we have copied the ngrok executable, run:

    ```
    ./ngrok http 9000
    ```

Running ./ngrok http 9000 will start a new tunnel between the local host and a public instance of ngrok server, and we should see the following:

```
ngrok by @inconshreveable

Session Status              online
Version                     2.2.4
Region                      United States (us)
Web Interface               http://127.0.0.1:4040
Forwarding                  http://add7231d.ngrok.io -> localhost:9000
Forwarding                  https://add7231d.ngrok.io -> localhost:9000

Connections                 ttl     opn     rt1     rt5     p50     p90
                            0       0       0.00    0.00    0.00    0.00
```

The forwarding URL changes every time you kill and restart `ngrok`. In the preceding case, the public URL of ngrok: `http://add7231d.ngrok.io` is mapped to my local server: `http://localhost:9000`. Isn't this easy?

To quickly test the public URL, open `web-app/src/app/app.global.ts` and update it, as follows:

```
export const Globals = Object.freeze({
    // BASE_API_URL: 'http://localhost:9000/',
    BASE_API_URL: 'https://add7231d.ngrok.io/',
    API_AUTH_TOKEN: 'AUTH_TOKEN',
    AUTH_USER: 'AUTH_USER'
});
```

Now, you can launch your web app from anywhere and it will talk to the API engine using the public URL.

 Do read the terms of service (`https://ngrok.com/tos`) and privacy policy (`https://ngrok.com/privacy`) of `ngrok` before proceeding further.

Defining the lambda function

Now that the voice model is trained and we have a public URL to access the API engine, we are going to write the required service to respond to the user's interactions.

When a user goes, *Alexa, ask smarty app the weather report*, Alexa will make a request to the AWS lambda function and the lambda function will call the API engine for appropriate activity.

Quoting from AWS: `https://aws.amazon.com/lambda/details/`

> *The AWS Lambda is a serverless compute service that runs your code in response to events and automatically manages the underlying compute resources for you. You can use AWS Lambda to extend other AWS services with custom logic, or create your own back-end services that operate at AWS scale, performance, and security.*

To know more about AWS lambda, refer to: `https://aws.amazon.com/lambda/details/`.

To get started, head to AWS console: `https://console.aws.amazon.com/` and select the region as North Virginia. As of today, AWS lambda services hosted in North America and Europe are only allowed to be linked with the Alexa Skill.

Next, from the **Service** menu on top, select **Lambda** under the **Compute** section. This will take us to the **Functions** screen of the lambda service. Click on **Create a Lambda function** and we will be asked to select a blueprint. Select **Blank Function**. Next, you will be asked to select a trigger; select **Alexa Skill Set**, as follows:

Click on **Next**. Now, we need to configure the function. Update it, as follows:

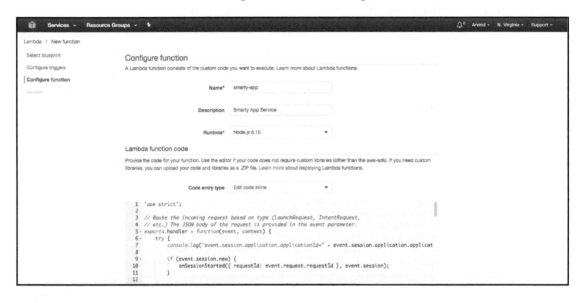

For **Lambda function code**, enter the following code:

```
'use strict';

// Route the incoming request based on type (LaunchRequest, IntentRequest,
// etc.) The JSON body of the request is provided in the event parameter.
exports.handler = function(event, context) {
    try {
        console.log("event.session.application.applicationId=" +
event.session.application.applicationId);

        if (event.session.new) {
            onSessionStarted({ requestId: event.request.requestId },
event.session);
        }

        if (event.request.type === "LaunchRequest") {
            onLaunch(event.request,
                event.session,
                function callback(sessionAttributes, speechletResponse) {
                    context.succeed(buildResponse(sessionAttributes,
speechletResponse));
                });
        } else if (event.request.type === "IntentRequest") {
            onIntent(event.request,
```

```
                    event.session,
                    function callback(sessionAttributes, speechletResponse) {
                        context.succeed(buildResponse(sessionAttributes,
speechletResponse));
                    });
        } else if (event.request.type === "SessionEndedRequest") {
            onSessionEnded(event.request, event.session);
            context.succeed();
        }
    } catch (e) {
        context.fail("Exception: " + e);
    }
};

/**
 * Called when the session starts.
 */
function onSessionStarted(sessionStartedRequest, session) {
    console.log("onSessionStarted requestId=" +
sessionStartedRequest.requestId + ", sessionId=" + session.sessionId);

    // add any session init logic here
}

/**
 * Called when the user invokes the skill without specifying what they
want.
 */
function onLaunch(launchRequest, session, callback) {
    console.log("onLaunch requestId=" + launchRequest.requestId + ",
sessionId=" + session.sessionId);

    var cardTitle = "Smarty App"
    var speechOutput = "Hello, What would you like to know about your farm
today?"
    callback(session.attributes,
        buildSpeechletResponse(cardTitle, speechOutput, "", true));
}

/**
 * Called when the user specifies an intent for this skill.
 */
function onIntent(intentRequest, session, callback) {
    console.log("onIntent requestId=" + intentRequest.requestId + ",
sessionId=" + session.sessionId);

    var intent = intentRequest.intent,
        intentName = intentRequest.intent.name;
```

```
    // dispatch custom intents to handlers here
    if (intentName == 'WeatherStatusIntent') {
        handleWSIRequest(intent, session, callback);
    } else if (intentName == 'ControlMotorIntent') {
        handleCMIRequest(intent, session, callback);
    } else {
        throw "Invalid intent";
    }
}

/**
 * Called when the user ends the session.
 * Is not called when the skill returns shouldEndSession=true.
 */
function onSessionEnded(sessionEndedRequest, session) {
    console.log("onSessionEnded requestId=" + sessionEndedRequest.requestId
+ ", sessionId=" + session.sessionId);

    // Add any cleanup logic here
}

function handleWSIRequest(intent, session, callback) {
    getData(function(speechOutput) {
        callback(session.attributes,
            buildSpeechletResponseWithoutCard(speechOutput, "", "true"));
    });
}

function handleCMIRequest(intent, session, callback) {
    var speechOutput = 'Got ';
    var status;
    var motorAction = intent.slots.motorAction.value;
    speechOutput += motorAction;
    if (motorAction === 'turn on') {
        status = 1;
    }

    if (motorAction === 'turn off') {
        status = 0;
    }
    setData(status, function(speechOutput) {
        callback(session.attributes,
            buildSpeechletResponseWithoutCard(speechOutput, "", "true"));
    });

}
```

```
function getData(cb) {
    var http = require('http');
    var chunk = '';
    var options = {
        host: '31d664cf.ngrok.io',
        port: 80,
        path: '/api/v1/data/b8:27:eb:39:92:0d/30',
        agent: false,
        timeout: 10000,
        method: 'GET',
        headers: {
            'AlexSkillRequest': true,
            'authorization': 'Bearer
eyJhbGciOiJIUzI1NiIsInR5cCI6IkpXVCJ9.eyJfaWQiOiI1OTFmZGI5ZGNlYjBiBiODM2YjIzMm
I3MjMiLCJpYXQiOjE0OTcxNjE4MTUsImV4cCI6MTQ5NzI0ODIxNX0.ua-SXAqLb-
XUEtbgY55TX_pKdD2Xj5OSM7b9Iox_Rd8'
        }
    };

    var req = http.request(options, function(res) {
        res.on('data', function(_chunk) {
            chunk += _chunk;
        });

        res.on('end', function() {
            var resp = chunk;
            if (typeof chunk === 'string') {
                resp = JSON.parse(chunk);
            }

            if (resp.length === 0) {
                cb('Looks like we have not gathered any data yet! Please
try again later!');
            }

            var d = resp[0].data;

            if (!d) {
                cb('Looks like there is something wrong with the data we
got! Please try again later!');
            }

            var temp = d.t || 'invalid';
            var humd = d.h || 'invalid';
            var mois = d.m || 'invalid';
            var rain = d.r || 'invalid';

            cb('The temperature is ' + temp + ' degrees celsius, the
```

```
humidity is ' + humd + ' percent, The moisture level is ' + mois + '
percent and the rain level is ' + rain + ' percent!');

        });

        res.on('error', function() {
            console.log(arguments);
            cb('Looks like something went wrong.');
        });
    });
    req.end();
}

function setData(status, cb) {
    var http = require('http');
    var chunk = '';
    var data = {
        'status': status,
        'macAddress': 'b8:27:eb:39:92:0d'
    };

    data = JSON.stringify(data);

    var options = {
        host: '31d664cf.ngrok.io',
        port: 80,
        path: '/api/v1/data',
        agent: false,
        timeout: 10000,
        method: 'POST',
        headers: {
            'AlexSkillRequest': true,
            'Content-Type': 'application/json',
            'Content-Length': Buffer.byteLength(data),
            'authorization': 'Bearer
eyJhbGciOiJIUzI1NiIsInR5cCI6IkpXVCJ9.eyJfaWQiOiI1OTFmZGI5ZGNlYjBiODM2YjIzMm
I3MjMiLCJpYXQiOjE0OTcxNjE4MTUsImV4cCI6MTQ5NzI0ODIxNX0.ua-SXAqLb-
XUEtbgY55TX_pKdD2Xj5OSM7b9Iox_Rd8'
        }
    };

    var req = http.request(options, function(res) {
        res.on('data', function(_chunk) {
            chunk += _chunk;
        });

        res.on('end', function() {
            var resp = chunk;
```

```
        if (typeof chunk === 'string') {
            resp = JSON.parse(chunk);
        }

        cb('Motor has been successfully ' + (status ? 'turned on' :
'turned off'));

    });

    res.on('error', function() {
        console.log(arguments);
        cb('Looks like something went wrong.');
    });
});

// post the data
req.write(data);
req.end();
}


// ------- Helper functions to build responses -------

function buildSpeechletResponse(title, output, repromptText,
shouldEndSession) {
    return {
        outputSpeech: {
            type: "PlainText",
            text: output
        },
        card: {
            type: "Simple",
            title: title,
            content: output
        },
        reprompt: {
            outputSpeech: {
                type: "PlainText",
                text: repromptText
            }
        },
        shouldEndSession: shouldEndSession
    };
}

function buildSpeechletResponseWithoutCard(output, repromptText,
shouldEndSession) {
    return {
```

```
            outputSpeech: {
                type: "PlainText",
                text: output
            },
            reprompt: {
                outputSpeech: {
                    type: "PlainText",
                    text: repromptText
                }
            },
            shouldEndSession: shouldEndSession
        };
    }

    function buildResponse(sessionAttributes, speechletResponse) {
        return {
            version: "1.0",
            sessionAttributes: sessionAttributes,
            response: speechletResponse
        };
    }
```

There is a lot going on in the code. `exports.handler()` is the default function that we need to set up for lambda to work. Inside that, we have defined the type of incoming request. And, if the incoming is an `IntentRequest`, we call `onIntent()`. Inside `onIntent()`, we fetch the `intentName` and invoke the appropriate logic.

If the `intentName` is `WeatherStatusIntent`, we invoke `handleWSIRequest()`, or else if the intentName is `ControlMotorIntent`, we call `handleCMIRequest()`.

Inside `handleWSIRequest()` we invoke the `getData()`, which will make a HTTP GET request to our `ngrok` URL. Once the data arrives, we construct a response and return it to the skill service.

And, `handleCMIRequest()` does the same, except it first gets the `motorAction` slot value and then calls `setData()`, which will call or either turn the motor on/off.

Once the code has been copied, you should find additional configuration at the bottom. We are going to leave the handler as-is. For the role, click on **Create a custom role**, and set it up, as follows:

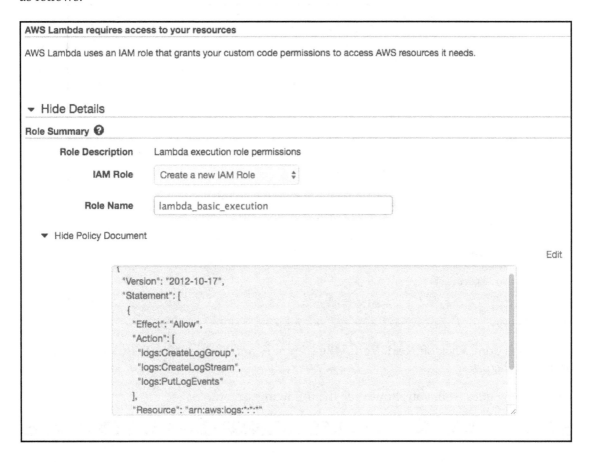

And click on **Allow**. This will create a new role that will get populated in **Existing role***, as follows:

Once this is done, click on **Next**. Verify the summary and click on **Create function** at the bottom of the page.

If everything goes well, you should see the following screen:

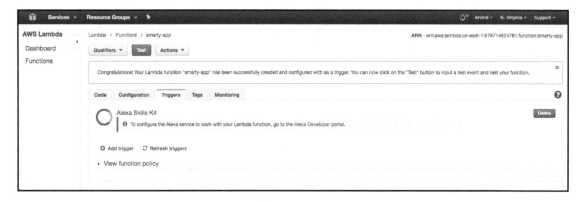

Do notice the **ARN** in the top right corner. This is the **Amazon Resource Name** (**ARN**) for our lambda function. We need to provide this as an input to the **Alexa Skills Kit**.

Deploying and testing

Now that we have all the pieces, we will configure the ARN in the Alexa skill we have created. Head back to Alexa skill and click on **Configuration**, and update the configuration as follows:

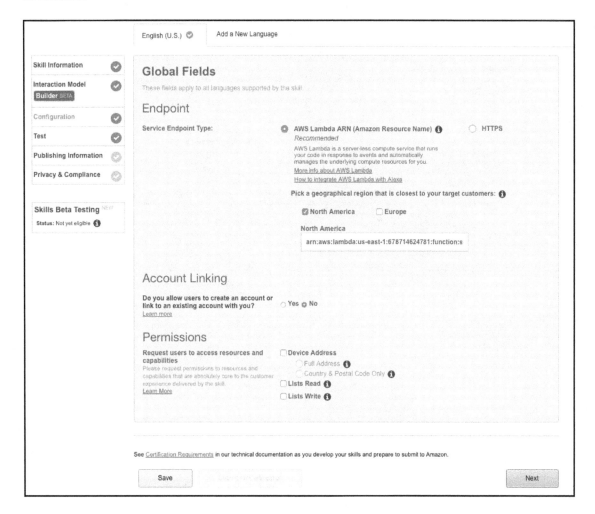

Click **Next**. If everything is set up correctly, we can test the setup.

Towards the bottom of the **Test** page, we should see a section named `Service Emulator`. You can test it, as follows:

The following screenshot shows the request received by lambda from Alexa:

With this, we are done with integrating Alexa with our IoT.js framework.

Summary

In this chapter, we have explored how to integrate a voice AI service such as Alexa with the IoTFW.js framework we have developed. We continued with the same example from Chapter 4, *Smart Agriculture*, and started off this chapter by setting up the relay that can turn the motor on/off. Next, we have understood how Alexa works. We have created a new custom skill and then set up the required voice model. After that, we have written the required business logic in AWS lambda, which will get the latest weather status as well as control the motor.

We have finally tested everything using the reverb app and also validated everything.

In Chapter 6, *Smart Wearable*, we are going to look at IoT and healthcare.

6
Smart Wearable

In this chapter, we are going to look at a simple healthcare application that can be created using Raspberry Pi 3. We are going to build a smart wearable with a 16x2 LCD that displays the location of the user, and also displays an accelerometer's values on the web/desktop/mobile interface. The target audience for this product would primarily be elderly people and the main use case being fall detection, which we are going to work with in Chapter 7, *Smart Wearable and IFTTT* .

We are going to look at the following in this chapter:

- IoT and healthcare
- Set up the required hardware
- Integrate the accelerometer and view live data

IoT and healthcare

Imagine a patient who successfully underwent a heart transplant surgery and is being sent home after post operational care in the hospital. The amount of attention on this patient would significantly reduce, as the facilities in the home would be minimal compared to a hospital. This is where IoT comes in with its real-time capability.

IoT and healthcare is a match made in heaven. The risks and rewards are equally high. Ability to monitor a patient's health in real time and get information about their pulse rate, body temperature, and other vital statistics, diagnose and act on it is quite precious. At the same time, if the connectivity was lost for two minutes, a life would be at stake.

In my opinion, to realize the full potential of IoT in healthcare, we may need to wait for another 5 - 10 years, where the connectivity is absolutely seamless and packet loss is a word of ancient history.

Smart wearable

As mentioned in the preceding section, we are going to do one of the critical things in healthcare using IoT. The main purpose of the smart wearable we are going to build is to identify fall detection. Once fall detection is identified, we notify the cloud about it. This is a very precious feature when we have elderly or sick people around who collapse due to unexpected reasons. Identifying the fall immediately and taking an action on it can be life saving at times.

To detect falls, we are going to use an accelerometer. Quoting from Wikipedia:

> "*An **accelerometer** is a device that measures proper acceleration. Proper acceleration, being the acceleration (or rate of change of velocity) of a body in its own instantaneous rest frame, is not the same as coordinate acceleration, being the acceleration in a fixed coordinate system. For example, an accelerometer at rest on the surface of the Earth will measure an acceleration due to Earth's gravity, straight upwards (by definition) of g ≈ 9.81 m/s2. By contrast, accelerometers in free fall (falling toward the centre of the Earth at a rate of about 9.81 m/s2) will measure zero.*"

To know more about an accelerometer and how it works, refer to *How an accelerometer works* at: `https://www.youtube.com/watch?v=i2U49usFo10`.

In this chapter, we are going to implement the basic system that gathers the X, Y, and Z axis acceleration raw values and gets displayed on web, desktop, and mobile apps. In `Chapter 7`, *Smart Wearable and IFTTT*, we are going to implement fall detection using these values.

Along with gathering the accelerometer values in real time, we are going to use the 16x2 LCD display to show the current time and the geolocation of the user. If needed, we can add other texts to this display as well. 16x2 is a simple interface to display content. This can be extended with Nokia 5110 LCD (`http://www.amazon.in/inch-Nokia-5110-KG075-KitsGuru/dp/B01CXNSJOA`) to have a more advanced display with graphics.

In the next section, we are going to put together the required hardware and then update the Raspberry Pi code. After that we are going to start working on the API engine and the UI templates.

Setting up smart wearable

The first thing to note about the hardware setup is that it is big and bulky. This is only a POC and is not even a remotely close production setup. The hardware setup would consist of an accelerometer connected to Raspberry Pi 3 and a 16X2 LCD.

The accelerometer ADXL345 gives the acceleration of X, Y, and Z axis over I2C protocol.

Connect the hardware as follows:

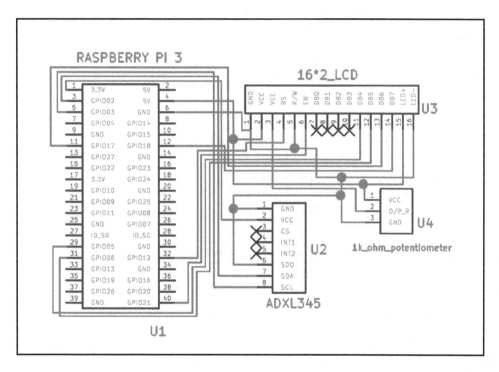

As you can see in the preceding schematic, we have made the following connections:

- Raspberry Pi and LCD:

Raspberry Pi number - Pin name	16x2 LCD Pi name
6 - GND - Breadboard rail 1	1 - GND
2 - 5V - Breadboard rail 2	2 - VCC
1 k Ohm potentiometer	3 - VEE

32 - GPIO 12	4 - RS
6 - GND - Breadboard rail 1	5 -R/W
40 - GPIO 21	6 - EN
NC	7 - DB0
NC	8 - DB1
NC	9 - DB2
NC	10 - DB3
29 - GPIO 5	11 - DB4
31 - GPIO 6	12 - DB5
11 - GPIO 17	13 - DB6
12 - GPIO 18	14 - DB7
2 - 5V - Breadboard rail 2	15 - LED+
6 - GND - Breadboard rail 1	16 - LED-

- Raspberry Pi and ADXL345:

Raspberry Pi number - Pin name	ADXL345 pin number - Pin name
1 - 3.3V	VCC
6 - GND - Breadboard rail 1	GND
5 - GPIO3/SCL1	SCL
3 - GPIO2/SDA1	SDA
6 - GND - Breadboard rail 1	SDO

We will add the required code:

1. First create a folder named `chapter6` and then copy the contents of `chapter4` into it. We will update this code as we go along

2. Now, we will start with the `pi-client`. On the Raspberry Pi, open `pi-client/index.js` and update it as follows:

```
var config = require('./config.js');
var mqtt = require('mqtt');
var GetMac = require('getmac');
var request = require('request');
var ADXL345 = require('adxl345-sensor');
require('events').EventEmitter.prototype._maxListeners = 100;

var adxl345 = new ADXL345(); // defaults to i2cBusNo 1,
i2cAddress 0x53

var Lcd = require('lcd'),
    lcd = new Lcd({
        rs: 12,
        e: 21,
        data: [5, 6, 17, 18],
        cols: 8,
        rows: 2
    });

var aclCtr = 0,
    locCtr = 0;

var x, prevX, y, prevY, z, prevZ;
var locationG; // global location variable

var client = mqtt.connect({
    port: config.mqtt.port,
    protocol: 'mqtts',
    host: config.mqtt.host,
    clientId: config.mqtt.clientId,
    reconnectPeriod: 1000,
    username: config.mqtt.clientId,
    password: config.mqtt.clientId,
    keepalive: 300,
    rejectUnauthorized: false
});

client.on('connect', function() {
    client.subscribe('rpi');
    client.subscribe('socket');
    GetMac.getMac(function(err, mac) {
        if (err) throw err;
        macAddress = mac;
        displayLocation();
```

```
            initADXL345();
            client.publish('api-engine', mac);
        });
    });

    client.on('message', function(topic, message) {
        message = message.toString();
        if (topic === 'rpi') {
            console.log('API Engine Response >> ', message);
        } else {
            console.log('Unknown topic', topic);
        }
    });

    function initADXL345() {
        adxl345.init().then(function() {
                console.log('ADXL345 initialization succeeded');
                // init loop after ADXL345 has been setup
                loop();
            })
            .catch(function(err) {
                console.error('ADXL345 initialization failed: ',
err);
            });
    }

    function loop() {
        // infinite loop, with 1 seconds delay
        setInterval(function() {
            // wait till we get the location
            // then start processing
            if (!locationG) return;

            if (aclCtr === 3) { // every 3 seconds
                aclCtr = 0;
                readSensorValues(function(acclVals) {
                    var x = acclVals.x;
                    var y = acclVals.y;
                    var z = acclVals.z;

                    var data2Send = {
                        data: {
                            acclVals: acclVals,
                            location: locationG
                        },
                        macAddress: macAddress
                    };
```

```
                    // no duplicate data
                    if (x !== prevX || y !== prevY || z !== prevZ)
{
                            console.log('data2Send', data2Send);
                            client.publish('accelerometer',
JSON.stringify(data2Send));
                            console.log('Data Published');
                            prevX = x;
                            prevY = y;
                            prevZ = z;
                    }
                });
            }

        if (locCtr === 300) { // every 300 seconds
            locCtr = 0;
            displayLocation();
        }

        aclCtr++;
        locCtr++;
    }, 1000); // every one second
}

function readSensorValues(CB) {
    adxl345.getAcceleration(true) // true for g-force units,
else false for m/s²
        .then(function(acceleration) {
            if (CB) CB(acceleration);
        })
        .catch((err) => {
            console.log('ADXL345 read error: ', err);
        });
}

function displayLocation() {
    request('http://ipinfo.io', function(error, res, body) {
        var info = JSON.parse(body);
        // console.log(info);
        locationG = info;
        var text2Print = '';
        text2Print += 'City: ' + info.city;
        text2Print += ' Region: ' + info.region;
        text2Print += ' Country: ' + info.country + ' ';
        lcd.setCursor(16, 0); // 1st row
        lcd.autoscroll();
        printScroll(text2Print);
    });
```

```
    }

    // a function to print scroll
    function printScroll(str, pos) {
        pos = pos || 0;

        if (pos === str.length) {
            pos = 0;
        }

        lcd.print(str[pos]);
        //console.log('printing', str[pos]);
        setTimeout(function() {
            return printScroll(str, pos + 1);
        }, 300);
    }

    // If ctrl+c is hit, free resources and exit.
    process.on('SIGINT', function() {
        lcd.clear();
        lcd.close();
        process.exit();
    });
```

As you can see from the preceding code, we are displaying the location, using `displayLocation()`, every one hour, as we are assuming that the location would not change frequently. We are using the `http://ipinfo.io/` service to get the user's location.

3. Finally, using `readSensorValues()` we get the value of `accelerometer` every 3 seconds and publish this data to a topic named `accelerometer`

4. Now, we will install the required dependencies. From inside the `pi-client` folder, run the following command:

    npm install async getmac adxl345-sensor mqtt request --save

5. Save all the files and start the mosca broker on the server or our desktop machine by running:

    mosca -c index.js -v | pino

6. Next, run the code on Raspberry Pi:

    npm start

This will start the `pi-client` and will start collecting the accelerometer and display the location on the LCD display as follows:

```
pi@raspberrypi: ~/Desktop/pi-client $ sudo node index.js
Found ADXL345 device id 0xe5 on bus i2c-1, address 0x53
ADXL345 initialization succeeded
data2Send { data:
   { acclVals: { x: -0.016, y: -0.064, z: -0.936, units: 'g' },
     location:
      { ip: '183.82.5.11',
        hostname: 'broadband.actcorp.in',
        city: 'Hyderabad',
        region: 'Telangana',
        country: 'IN',
        loc: '17.3753,78.4744',
        org: 'AS18209 Atria Convergence Technologies pvt ltd' } },
  macAddress: 'b8:27:eb:39:92:0d' }
Data Published
```

My setup is shown as follows:

Next, we will work with the API engine.

Updating the API engine

Now that we have the smart wearable running and sending the three axis data, we will now implement the required logic needed to accept that data in the API engine and send the data to the web/desktop/mobile app:

Open `api-engine/server/mqtt/index.js` and update it as follows:

```javascript
var Data = require('../api/data/data.model');
var mqtt = require('mqtt');
var config = require('../config/environment');
var client = mqtt.connect({
    port: config.mqtt.port,
    protocol: 'mqtts',
    host: config.mqtt.host,
    clientId: config.mqtt.clientId,
    reconnectPeriod: 1000,
    username: config.mqtt.clientId,
    password: config.mqtt.clientId,
    keepalive: 300,
    rejectUnauthorized: false
});

client.on('connect', function() {
    console.log('Connected to Mosca at ' + config.mqtt.host + ' on port ' +
config.mqtt.port);
    client.subscribe('api-engine');
    client.subscribe('accelerometer');
});

client.on('message', function(topic, message) {
    // message is Buffer
    // console.log('Topic >> ', topic);
    // console.log('Message >> ', message.toString());
    if (topic === 'api-engine') {
        var macAddress = message.toString();
        console.log('Mac Address >> ', macAddress);
        client.publish('rpi', 'Got Mac Address: ' + macAddress);
    } else if (topic === 'accelerometer') {
        var data = JSON.parse(message.toString());
        // create a new data record for the device
        Data.create(data, function(err, data) {
            if (err) return console.error(err);
            // if the record has been saved successfully,
            // websockets will trigger a message to the web-app
            console.log('Data Saved :', data.data);
        });
```

```
    } else {
        console.log('Unknown topic', topic);
    }
});
```

Here, we are subscribing to a topic named `accelerometer` and listening for changes on it. Next, we update `api-engine/server/api/data/data.controller.js` as follows:

```javascript
'use strict';

var Data = require('./data.model');

/**
 * Get Data for a device
 */
exports.index = function(req, res) {
    var macAddress = req.params.deviceId;
    var limit = parseInt(req.params.limit) || 30;
    Data
        .find({
            macAddress: macAddress
        })
        .sort({ 'createdAt': -1 })
        .limit(limit)
        .exec(function(err, data) {
            if (err) return res.status(500).send(err);
            res.status(200).json(data);
        });
};

/**
 * Create a new data record
 */
exports.create = function(req, res, next) {
    var data = req.body || {};
    data.createdBy = req.user._id;

    Data.create(data, function(err, _data) {
        if (err) return res.status(500).send(err);
        return res.json(_data);
    });
};
```

The preceding code is used to save the data to database and fetch the data from database when requested from web, desktop, and mobile apps.

Save all the files and run the API engine:

```
npm start
```

This will start the API engine, if needed we can restart the smart wearable and we should see the following:

```
[→ api-engine npm start

> api-engine@0.1.0 start /Users/arvindravulavaru/Arvind/Books/Advanced IoT with JS/FD/code/chapter6/api-engine
> nodemon server/app.js

[nodemon] 1.10.0
[nodemon] to restart at any time, enter `rs`
[nodemon] watching: *.*
[nodemon] starting `node server/app.js`
Express server listening on 9000, in development mode
Connected to Mosca at 127.0.0.1 on port 8883
Mac Address >>  b8:27:eb:39:92:0d
data >>  { data:
   { acclVals: { x: -0.016, y: -0.064, z: -0.936, units: 'g' },
     location:
      { ip: '183.82.5.11',
        hostname: 'broadband.actcorp.in',
        city: 'Hyderabad',
        region: 'Telangana',
        country: 'IN',
        loc: '17.3753,78.4744',
        org: 'AS18209 Atria Convergence Technologies pvt ltd' } },
  macAddress: 'b8:27:eb:39:92:0d' }
```

In the next section, we will work on the web app to display the data.

Updating the web app

Now that we are done with the API engine, we will update the template in the web app to display the three axis data. Open `web-app/src/app/device/device.component.html` and update it as follows:

```html
<div class="container">
  <br>
  <div *ngIf="!device">
    <h3 class="text-center">Loading!</h3>
  </div>
  <div class="row" *ngIf="lastRecord">
    <div class="col-md-12">
      <div class="panel panel-info">
        <div class="panel-heading">
          <h3 class="panel-title">
                      {{device.name}}
                </h3>
```

```
            <span class="pull-right btn-click">
                        <i class="fa fa-chevron-circle-up"></i>
                    </span>
        </div>
        <div class="clearfix"></div>
        <div class="table-responsive">
          <table class="table table-striped">
            <tr *ngIf="lastRecord">
              <td>X-Axis</td>
              <td>{{lastRecord.data.acclVals.x}}
{{lastRecord.data.acclVals.units}}</td>
            </tr>
            <tr *ngIf="lastRecord">
              <td>Y-Axis</td>
              <td>{{lastRecord.data.acclVals.y}}
{{lastRecord.data.acclVals.units}}</td>
            </tr>
            <tr *ngIf="lastRecord">
              <td>Z-Axis</td>
              <td>{{lastRecord.data.acclVals.z}}
{{lastRecord.data.acclVals.units}}</td>
            </tr>
            <tr *ngIf="lastRecord">
              <td>Location</td>
              <td>{{lastRecord.data.location.city}},
{{lastRecord.data.location.region}},
{{lastRecord.data.location.country}}</td>
            </tr>
            <tr *ngIf="lastRecord">
              <td>Received At</td>
              <td>{{lastRecord.createdAt | date : 'medium'}}</td>
            </tr>
          </table>
          <hr>
          <div class="col-md-12" *ngIf="acclVals.length > 0">
          <canvas baseChart [datasets]="acclVals"
[labels]="lineChartLabels" [options]="lineChartOptions"
[legend]="lineChartLegend" [chartType]="lineChartType"></canvas>
          </div>
        </div>
      </div>
    </div>
  </div>
</div>
```

The required logic will be inside `device.component.ts`. Open `web-app/src/app/device/device.component.ts` and update it as follows:

```
import { Component, OnInit, OnDestroy } from '@angular/core';
import { DevicesService } from '../services/devices.service';
import { Params, ActivatedRoute } from '@angular/router';
import { SocketService } from '../services/socket.service';
import { DataService } from '../services/data.service';
import { NotificationsService } from 'angular2-notifications';

@Component({
  selector: 'app-device',
  templateUrl: './device.component.html',
  styleUrls: ['./device.component.css']
})
export class DeviceComponent implements OnInit, OnDestroy {
  device: any;
  data: Array<any>;
  toggleState: boolean = false;
  private subDevice: any;
  private subData: any;
  lastRecord: any;

  // line chart config
  public lineChartOptions: any = {
    responsive: true,
    legend: {
      position: 'bottom',
    }, hover: {
      mode: 'label'
    }, scales: {
      xAxes: [{
        display: true,
        scaleLabel: {
          display: true,
          labelString: 'Time'
        }
      }],
      yAxes: [{
        display: true,
        ticks: {
          beginAtZero: true,
          // steps: 10,
          // stepValue: 5,
          // max: 70
        }
      }],
```

```
    zAxes: [{
      display: true,
      ticks: {
        beginAtZero: true,
        // steps: 10,
        // stepValue: 5,
        // max: 70
      }
    }]
  },
  title: {
    display: true,
    text: 'X,Y,Z vs. Time'
  }
};

public lineChartLegend: boolean = true;
public lineChartType: string = 'line';
public acclVals: Array<any> = [];
public lineChartLabels: Array<any> = [];

constructor(private deviceService: DevicesService,
  private socketService: SocketService,
  private dataService: DataService,
  private route: ActivatedRoute,
  private notificationsService: NotificationsService) { }

ngOnInit() {
  this.subDevice = this.route.params.subscribe((params) => {
    this.deviceService.getOne(params['id']).subscribe((response) => {
      this.device = response.json();
      this.getData();
    });
  });
}

getData() {
  this.dataService.get(this.device.macAddress).subscribe((response) => {
    this.data = response.json();
    this.lastRecord = this.data[0]; // descending order data
    this.toggleState = this.lastRecord.data.s;
    this.genChart();
    this.socketInit();
  });
}

socketInit() {
  this.subData =
```

```
this.socketService.getData(this.device.macAddress).subscribe((data) => {
    if (this.data.length <= 0) return;
    this.data.splice(this.data.length - 1, 1); // remove the last record
    this.data.push(data); // add the new one
    this.lastRecord = data;
    this.toggleState = this.lastRecord.data.s;
    this.genChart();
  });
}

ngOnDestroy() {
  this.subDevice.unsubscribe();
  this.subData ? this.subData.unsubscribe() : '';
}

genChart() {
  let data = this.data;
  let _acclVals: Array<any> = [];
  let _lblArr: Array<any> = [];

  let xArr: Array<any> = [];
  let yArr: Array<any> = [];
  let zArr: Array<any> = [];
  for (var i = 0; i < data.length; i++) {
    let _d = data[i];
    xArr.push(_d.data.acclVals.x);
    yArr.push(_d.data.acclVals.y);
    zArr.push(_d.data.acclVals.z);
    _lblArr.push(this.formatDate(_d.createdAt));
  }

  // reverse data to show the latest on the right side
  xArr.reverse();
  yArr.reverse();
  zArr.reverse();
  _lblArr.reverse();

  _acclVals = [
    {
      data: xArr,
      label: 'X-Axis'
    },
    {
      data: yArr,
      label: 'Y-Axis'
    },
    {
      data: zArr,
```

```
        label: 'Z-Axis'
      }
    ]

    this.acclVals = _acclVals;

    this.lineChartLabels = _lblArr;
  }

  private formatDate(originalTime) {
    var d = new Date(originalTime);
    var datestring = d.getDate() + "-" + (d.getMonth() + 1) + "-" +
d.getFullYear() + " " +
      d.getHours() + ":" + d.getMinutes();
    return datestring;
  }

}
```

Save all the files and run the following command:

npm start

Navigate to `http://localhost:4200` and view the device and we should see the following:

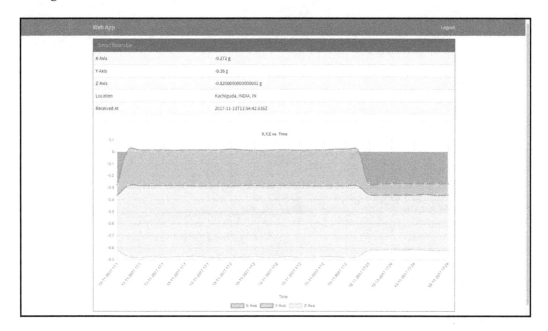

With this, we are done with the web app.

Updating a desktop app

Now that the web app is done, we are going to build the same and deploy it inside our desktop app.

To get started, head back to the terminal/prompt of the `web-app` folder and run:

```
ng build --env=prod
```

And this will create a new folder inside the `web-app` folder named `dist`. The contents of the `dist` folder should be similar to the following:

```
.
├── favicon.ico
├── index.html
├── inline.bundle.js
├── inline.bundle.js.map
├── main.bundle.js
├── main.bundle.js.map
├── polyfills.bundle.js
├── polyfills.bundle.js.map
├── scripts.bundle.js
├── scripts.bundle.js.map
├── styles.bundle.js
├── styles.bundle.js.map
├── vendor.bundle.js
└── vendor.bundle.js.map
```

All the code we have written is finally bundled into the preceding files. We will grab all the files (not the `dist` folder) present inside the `dist` folder and then paste it inside the `desktop-app/app` folder. The final structure of the desktop app after the preceding changes will be as follows:

```
.

├─── app
│    ├─── favicon.ico
│    ├─── index.html
│    ├─── inline.bundle.js
│    ├─── inline.bundle.js.map
│    ├─── main.bundle.js
│    ├─── main.bundle.js.map
│    ├─── polyfills.bundle.js
│    ├─── polyfills.bundle.js.map
│    ├─── scripts.bundle.js
│    ├─── scripts.bundle.js.map
│    ├─── styles.bundle.js
│    ├─── styles.bundle.js.map
│    ├─── vendor.bundle.js
│    └─── vendor.bundle.js.map
├─── freeport.js
├─── index.css
├─── index.html
├─── index.js
├─── license
```

```
├──── package.json

├──── readme.md

└──── server.js
```

To test drive, run the following:

```
npm start
```

And then when we navigate to the **VIEW DEVICE** page, we should see the following screen:

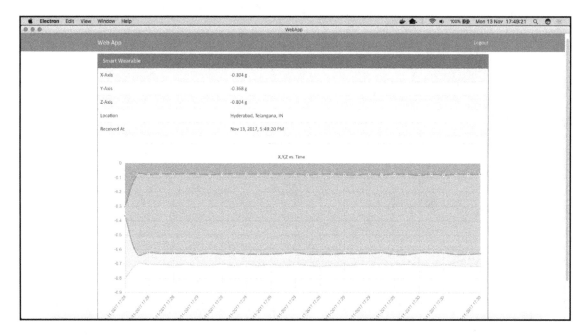

With this we are done with the development of the desktop app. In the next section, we will update the mobile app.

Updating the mobile app template

In the last section, we have updated the desktop app. In this section, we are going to update the mobile app template to display the three axis data.

First we are going to update the view-device template. Update `mobile-app/src/pages/view-device/view-device.html` as follows:

```
<ion-header>
    <ion-navbar>
        <ion-title>Mobile App</ion-title>
    </ion-navbar>
</ion-header>
<ion-content padding>
    <div *ngIf="!lastRecord">
        <h3 class="text-center">Loading!</h3>
    </div>
    <div *ngIf="lastRecord">
        <ion-list>
            <ion-item>
                <ion-label>Name</ion-label>
                <ion-label>{{device.name}}</ion-label>
            </ion-item>
            <ion-item>
                <ion-label>X-Axis</ion-label>
                <ion-label>{{lastRecord.data.acclVals.x}}
{{lastRecord.data.acclVals.units}}</ion-label>
            </ion-item>
            <ion-item>
                <ion-label>Y-Axis</ion-label>
                <ion-label>{{lastRecord.data.acclVals.y}}
{{lastRecord.data.acclVals.units}}</ion-label>
            </ion-item>
            <ion-item>
                <ion-label>Z-Axis</ion-label>
                <ion-label>{{lastRecord.data.acclVals.z}}
{{lastRecord.data.acclVals.units}}</ion-label>
            </ion-item>
            <ion-item>
                <ion-label>Location</ion-label>
                <ion-label>{{lastRecord.data.location.city}},
{{lastRecord.data.location.region}},
{{lastRecord.data.location.country}}</ion-label>
            </ion-item>
            <ion-item>
                <ion-label>Received At</ion-label>
                <ion-label>{{lastRecord.createdAt | date: 'medium'}}</ion-label>
            </ion-item>
        </ion-list>
    </div>
</ion-content>
```

Next, we update `mobile-app/src/pages/view-device/view-device.ts` as follows:

```typescript
import { Component } from '@angular/core';
import { IonicPage, NavController, NavParams } from 'ionic-angular';

import { DevicesService } from '../../services/device.service';
import { DataService } from '../../services/data.service';
import { ToastService } from '../../services/toast.service';
import { SocketService } from '../../services/socket.service';

@IonicPage()
@Component({
    selector: 'page-view-device',
    templateUrl: 'view-device.html',
})
export class ViewDevicePage {
    device: any;
    data: Array<any>;
    toggleState: boolean = false;
    private subData: any;
    lastRecord: any;


    constructor(private navCtrl: NavController,
            private navParams: NavParams,
            private socketService: SocketService,
            private deviceService: DevicesService,
            private dataService: DataService,
            private toastService: ToastService) {
            this.device = navParams.get("device");
            console.log(this.device);
    }

    ionViewDidLoad() {
            this.deviceService.getOne(this.device._id).subscribe((response) =>
{
                this.device = response.json();
                this.getData();
                this.socketInit();
            });
    }

    getData() {
            this.dataService.get(this.device.macAddress).subscribe((response)
=> {
                this.data = response.json();
                this.lastRecord = this.data[0]; // descending order data
```

```
        });
    }
    socketInit() {
        this.subData =
this.socketService.getData(this.device.macAddress).subscribe((data) => {
            if (this.data.length <= 0) return;
            this.data.splice(this.data.length - 1, 1); // remove the
last record
            this.data.push(data); // add the new one
            this.lastRecord = data;
        });
    }

    ionViewDidUnload() {
        this.subData && this.subData.unsubscribe &&
this.subData.unsubscribe(); //unsubscribe if subData is defined
    }
}
```

Save all the files and run the mobile app either by using `ionic serve` or `ionic cordova run android`.

And we should see the following:

With this we are done with displaying the data from the smart wearable on the mobile app.

Summary

In this chapter, we have seen how to build a simple smart wearable using Raspberry Pi 3. We have set up a LCD and a three-axis accelerometer and we displayed the location information on the display. We have posted the accelerometer data in real time to the cloud and displayed it on the web, desktop, and mobile apps.

In Chapter 7, *Smart Wearable and IFTTT*, we are going to take the smart wearable to the next level by implementing IFTTT rules on top of it. We are going to perform actions such as making a phone call or sending an SMS to the patience emergency contact so that immediate care can be given.

7
Smart Wearable and IFTTT

In Chapter 6, *Smart Wearable,* we looked at how to build a simple wearable that displays a user's location and also reads accelerometer values. In this chapter, we are going to take that application to the next level by implementing fall detection logic on the device and then adding **If This Then That** (**IFTTT**) rules on top of the data to execute actions when certain events happen. We will look at the following topics:

- What is IFTTT
- IFTTT and IoT
- Understanding fall detection
- Accelerometer-based fall detection
- Building an IFTTT rules engine

IFTTT and IoT

This reactive pattern can be easily applied to certain situations. For example, if a patient falls down, then call an ambulance, or if the temperature goes below 15 degrees, then turn off the AC, and so on. These are simple rules that we define that can help us automate a lot of processes.

In IoT, rules engines are key to automating most monotonous tasks. In this chapter, we are going to build a simple hardcoded rules engine that will continuously monitor the incoming data. If the incoming data matches any of our rules, it will execute a response.

What we are building is a similar concept to `ifttt.com` (`https://ifttt.com/discover`), but is very specific to IoT devices that are present inside our framework. IFTTT (`https://ifttt.com/discover`) has no relation to what we are building in our book.

Fall detection

In `Chapter 6`, *Smart Wearable*, we gathered three axis values from the accelerometer. Now, we are going to make use of this data to detect falls.

I would recommend watching the video *Accelerometer in Freefall* (`https://www.youtube.com/watch?v=-om0eTXsgnY`), which explains how an accelerometer behaves both when it is stationary and in motion.

Now that we understand the basic concept of fall detection, let's talk about our specific use case.

The biggest challenge in fall detection is to distinguish falling from other activities, such as running and jumping. In this chapter, we are going to keep things simple and work on very basic conditions, where a user at rest or in constant motion suddenly falls down.

To identify whether the user has fallen down, we use the signal magnitude vector or *SMV*. *SMV* is the root mean square of the values of the three axes. That is:

$$SMV = \sqrt{x^2 + y^2 + z^2}$$

If we start plotting the **SMV** over **Time** for a user who is standing idle and then falls down, we will end up with a graph, as follows:

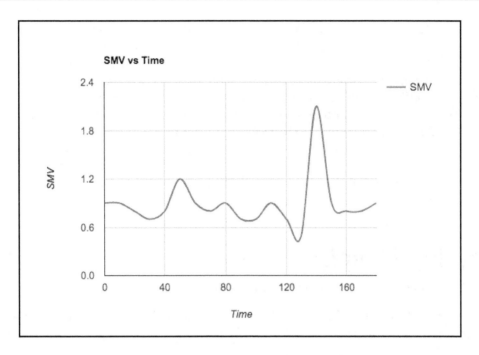

Note the spike at the end of the chart. This is the point at which the user actually fell.

Now, when we gather the accelerometer values from ADXL345, we will calculate the SMV. Based on multiple iterations using the smart wearable we have built, I was consistently able to detect falls at an SMV value of 1 g. For anything less than 1 g SMV, the user is almost always considered to be stationary and anything greater than 1 g SMV is considered a fall.

Do note that I have placed the accelerometer in such a way that the y-axis is perpendicular to the ground.

Once we put the setup together , you can see for yourself how the SMV values change with a change in the accelerometer's position.

Do note that if you are performing other activities, such as jumping or squatting, the fall detection might be triggered. You can play around with the threshold value of 1 g SMV to get consistent fall detection.

You can also refer to *Detecting Human Falls with a 3-Axis Digital Accelerometer*: (`http://www.analog.com/en/analog-dialogue/articles/ detecting-falls-3-axis-digital-accelerometer.html`), or *Accelerometer-based on-body sensor localization for health and medical monitoring applications* (`https://www.ncbi.nlm.nih.gov/pmc/articles/ PMC3279922/`), and *Development of the Algorithm for Detecting Falls during Daily Activity using 2 Tri-Axial Accelerometers* (`http://waset.org/ publications/2993/development-of-the-algorithm-for-detecting- falls-during-daily-activity-using-2-tri-axial-accelerometers`) to get a greater understanding of this topic and improve the efficiency of the system.

Updating Raspberry Pi

Now that we know what needs to be done, we will get started with the code.

Before we proceed, create a folder named `chapter7` and make a copy of the `chapter6` code in the `chapter7` folder.

Next, open the `pi/index.js` file. We will update the ADXL345 initialization setup and then start working with the values. Update `pi/index.js`, as follows:

```
var config = require('./config.js');
var mqtt = require('mqtt');
var GetMac = require('getmac');
var request = require('request');
var ADXL345 = require('adxl345-sensor');
require('events').EventEmitter.prototype._maxListeners = 100;

var adxl345 = new ADXL345(); // defaults to i2cBusNo 1, i2cAddress 0x53

var Lcd = require('lcd'),
    lcd = new Lcd({
        rs: 12,
        e: 21,
        data: [5, 6, 17, 18],
        cols: 8,
        rows: 2
    });

var aclCtr = 0,
    locCtr = 0;
```

```
var prevX, prevY, prevZ, prevSMV, prevFALL;
var locationG; // global location variable

var client = mqtt.connect({
    port: config.mqtt.port,
    protocol: 'mqtts',
    host: config.mqtt.host,
    clientId: config.mqtt.clientId,
    reconnectPeriod: 1000,
    username: config.mqtt.clientId,
    password: config.mqtt.clientId,
    keepalive: 300,
    rejectUnauthorized: false
});

client.on('connect', function() {
    client.subscribe('rpi');
    client.subscribe('socket');
    GetMac.getMac(function(err, mac) {
        if (err) throw err;
        macAddress = mac;
        displayLocation();
        initADXL345();
        client.publish('api-engine', mac);
    });
});

client.on('message', function(topic, message) {
    message = message.toString();
    if (topic === 'rpi') {
        console.log('API Engine Response >> ', message);
    } else {
        console.log('Unknown topic', topic);
    }
});

function initADXL345() {
    adxl345.init()
        .then(() => adxl345.setMeasurementRange(ADXL345.RANGE_2_G()))
        .then(() => adxl345.setDataRate(ADXL345.DATARATE_100_HZ()))
        .then(() => adxl345.setOffsetX(0)) // measure for your particular
device
        .then(() => adxl345.setOffsetY(0)) // measure for your particular
device
        .then(() => adxl345.setOffsetZ(0)) // measure for your particular
device
        .then(() => adxl345.getMeasurementRange())
        .then((range) => {
```

```
                    console.log('Measurement range:',
ADXL345.stringifyMeasurementRange(range));
            return adxl345.getDataRate();
        })
        .then((rate) => {
            console.log('Data rate: ', ADXL345.stringifyDataRate(rate));
            return adxl345.getOffsets();
        })
        .then((offsets) => {
            console.log('Offsets: ', JSON.stringify(offsets, null, 2));
            console.log('ADXL345 initialization succeeded');
            loop();
        })
        .catch((err) => console.error('ADXL345 initialization failed:',
err));
}

function loop() {
    // infinite loop, with 3 seconds delay
    setInterval(function() {
        // wait till we get the location
        // then start processing
        if (!locationG) return;

        readSensorValues(function(acclVals) {
            var x = acclVals.x;
            var y = acclVals.y;
            var z = acclVals.z;
            var fall = 0;
            var smv = Math.sqrt(x * x, y * y, z * z);

            if (smv > 1) {
                fall = 1;
            }

            acclVals.smv = smv;
            acclVals.fall = fall;

            var data2Send = {
                data: {
                    acclVals: acclVals,
                    location: locationG
                },
                macAddress: macAddress
            };

            // no duplicate data
            if (fall === 1 && (x !== prevX || y !== prevY || z !== prevZ ||
```

```
smv !== prevSMV || fall !== prevFALL)) {
                console.log('Fall Detected >> ', acclVals);
                client.publish('accelerometer', JSON.stringify(data2Send));
                console.log('Data Published');
                prevX = x;
                prevY = y;
                prevZ = z;
            }
        });

        if (locCtr === 600) { // every 5 mins
            locCtr = 0;
            displayLocation();
        }

        aclCtr++;
        locCtr++;
    }, 500); // every one second
}

function readSensorValues(CB) {
    adxl345.getAcceleration(true) // true for g-force units, else false for
m/s²
        .then(function(acceleration) {
            if (CB) CB(acceleration);
        })
        .catch((err) => {
            console.log('ADXL345 read error: ', err);
        });
}

function displayLocation() {
    request('http://ipinfo.io', function(error, res, body) {
        var info = JSON.parse(body);
        // console.log(info);
        locationG = info;
        var text2Print = '';
        text2Print += 'City: ' + info.city;
        text2Print += ' Region: ' + info.region;
        text2Print += ' Country: ' + info.country + ' ';
        lcd.setCursor(16, 0); // 1st row
        lcd.autoscroll();
        printScroll(text2Print);
    });
}

// a function to print scroll
function printScroll(str, pos) {
```

```
    pos = pos || 0;

    if (pos === str.length) {
        pos = 0;
    }

    lcd.print(str[pos]);
    //console.log('printing', str[pos]);

    setTimeout(function() {
        return printScroll(str, pos + 1);
    }, 300);
}

// If ctrl+c is hit, free resources and exit.
process.on('SIGINT', function() {
    lcd.clear();
    lcd.close();
    process.exit();
});
```

Note `initADXL345()`. We define the measurement range as 2_G, clear the offsets, and then we invoke the infinite loop function. In this scenario, we run the `setInterval()` every 500 ms instead of every 1 second. `readSensorValues()` is invoked every 500 ms instead of every 3 seconds. This is to make sure that we capture falls without much delay.

In the `readSensorValues()`, once the x, y, and z values are available, we calculate the SMV. Then, we check whether the SMV value is greater than 1: if it is, then we have detected a fall.

Along with the x, y, and z values, we send the SMV value as well as the fall value to the API engine. Also, do note that in this example, we are not sending all values as we collect them. We send data only if the fall is detected.

Save all of the files. Start the broker by running the following command from the `chapter7/broker` folder:

```
mosca -c index.js -v | pino
```

Next, start the API engine by running the following command from the `chapter7/api-engine` folder:

npm start

We are yet to add the IFTTT logic to the API engine, which we will do in the next section. For now, to validate our setup, let's run the `index.js` file on the Raspberry Pi by executing:

npm start

If everything goes well, the accelerometer should be initialized successfully and the data should start coming in.

If we simulate a free fall, we should see our first piece of data going to the API engine, and it should look something like the following screenshot:

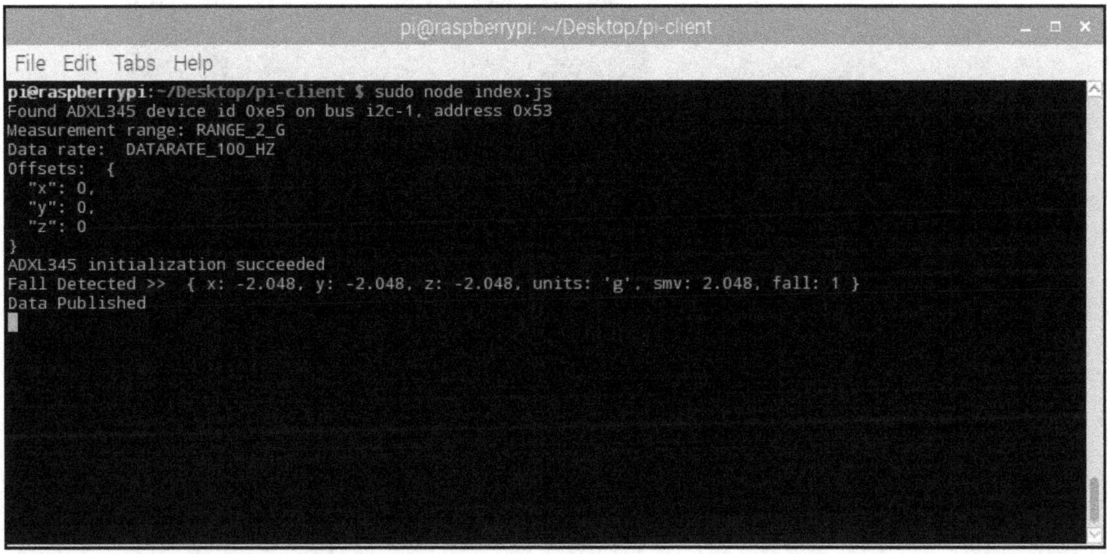

As you can see, the simulated free fall gave an SMV of `2.048` g.

My hardware setup is as shown here:

I have glued the entire setup to a **Styrofoam** sheet, so I can comfortably test the fall detection logic.

 I removed the 16 x 2 LCD from the setup while I was identifying the SMV for free fall.

In the next section, we are going to read the data that we received from the device and then execute rules based on it.

Building the IFTTT rules engine

Now that we are sending the required data to the API engine, we will be doing two things:

1. Showing data that we got from the smart wearable on the web, desktop, and mobile apps
2. Executing rules on top of the data

We will get started with the second objective first. We will be building a rules engine to execute rules based on the data we have received.

Let's get started by creating a folder named `ifttt` at the root of the `api-engine/server` folder. Inside the `ifttt` folder, create a file named `rules.json`. Update `api-engine/server/ifttt/rules.json`, as follows:

```
[{
    "device": "b8:27:eb:39:92:0d",
    "rules": [
    {
        "if":
        {
            "prop": "fall",
            "cond": "eq",
            "valu": 1
        },
        "then":
        {
            "action": "EMAIL",
            "to": "arvind.ravulavaru@gmail.com"
        }
    }]
}]
```

As you can see from the preceding code, we are maintaining a JSON file with all of our rules. In our scenario, we have only one rule for one device, and the rule has two parts: the `if` part and the `then` part. The `if` refers to the property, which needs to be checked against the incoming data, the checking condition, and the value against which it needs to be checked. The `then` part refers to the action that needs to be taken if the `if` matches. In the preceding case, this action involves sending an email.

Next, we are going to build the rules engine itself. Create a file named `ifttt.js` inside the `api-engine/server/ifttt` **folder and update** `api-engine/server/ifttt/ifttt.js`, as follows:

```javascript
var Rules = require('./rules.json');

exports.processData = function(data) {

    for (var i = 0; i < Rules.length; i++) {
        if (Rules[i].device === data.macAddress) {
            // the rule belows to the incoming device's data
            for (var j = 0; j < Rules[i].rules.length; j++) {
                // process one rule at a time
                var rule = Rules[i].rules[j];
                var data = data.data.acclVals;
                if (checkRuleAndData(rule, data)) {
                    console.log('Rule Matched', 'Processing Then.');
                    if (rule.then.action === 'EMAIL') {
                        console.log('Sending email to', rule.then.to);
                        EMAIL(rule.then.to);
                    } else {
                        console.log('Unknown Then! Please re-check the
rules');
                    }
                } else {
                    console.log('Rule Did Not Matched', rule, data);
                }
            }
        }
    }
}

/*   Rule process Helper   */
function checkRuleAndData(rule, data) {
    var rule = rule.if;
    if (rule.cond === 'lt') {
        return rule.valu < data[rule['prop']];
    } else if (rule.cond === 'lte') {
        return rule.valu <= data[rule['prop']];
    } else if (rule.cond === 'eq') {
        return rule.valu === data[rule['prop']];
    } else if (rule.cond === 'gte') {
        return rule.valu >= data[rule['prop']];
    } else if (rule.cond === 'gt') {
        return rule.valu > data[rule['prop']];
    } else if (rule.cond === 'ne') {
        return rule.valu !== data[rule['prop']];
```

```
    } else {
        return false;
    }
}


/*Then Helpers*/
function SMS() {
    /// AN EXAMPLE TO SHOW OTHER THENs
}

function CALL() {
    /// AN EXAMPLE TO SHOW OTHER THENs
}

function PUSHNOTIFICATION() {
    /// AN EXAMPLE TO SHOW OTHER THENs
}

function EMAIL(to) {
    /// AN EXAMPLE TO SHOW OTHER THENs
    var email = require('emailjs');
    var server = email.server.connect({
        user: 'arvind.ravulavaru@gmail.com',
        password: 'XXXXXXXXXX',
        host: 'smtp.gmail.com',
        ssl: true
    });

    server.send({
        text: 'Fall has been detected. Please attend to the patient',
        from: 'Patient Bot <arvind.ravulavaru@gmail.com>',
        to: to,
        subject: 'Fall Alert!!'
    }, function(err, message) {
        if (err) {
            console.log('Message sending failed!', err);
        }
    });
}
```

The logic is quite simple. processData() gets called when a new data record comes to the API engine. Then, we load all of the rules from the rules.json file and we iterate over them to check whether or not the current rule is meant for the incoming device.

If yes, then `checkRuleAndData()` is called by passing the rule and incoming data to check whether the current data set matches any of the predefined rules. If it does, we check the action, which in our case is the sending of an email. You can update the appropriate email credentials in the code.

Once this is done, we need to invoke `processData()` from `api-engine/server/mqtt/index.js` `client.on('message')` with the `topic` equaling `accelerometer`.

Update `client.on('message')`, as follows:

```
client.on('message', function(topic, message) {
    // message is Buffer
    // console.log('Topic >> ', topic);
    // console.log('Message >> ', message.toString());
    if (topic === 'api-engine') {
        var macAddress = message.toString();
        console.log('Mac Address >> ', macAddress);
        client.publish('rpi', 'Got Mac Address: ' + macAddress);
    } else if (topic === 'accelerometer') {
        var data = JSON.parse(message.toString());
        console.log('data >> ', data);
        // create a new data record for the device
        Data.create(data, function(err, data) {
            if (err) return console.error(err);
            // if the record has been saved successfully,
            // websockets will trigger a message to the web-app
            // console.log('Data Saved :', data.data);
            // Invoke IFTTT Rules Engine
            RulesEngine.processData(data);
        });
    } else {
        console.log('Unknown topic', topic);
    }
});
```

That is it. We have all the pieces needed for the IFTTT engine to run.

Save all of the files and restart the API engine. Now, simulate a fall and we should see an email coming our way, which should look something like this:

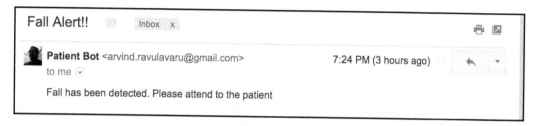

Now that we are done with the IFTTT engine, we will update the interfaces to reflect the new data we have gathered.

Updating the web app

To update the web app, open `web-app/src/app/device/device.component.html` and update it, as follows:

```html
<div class="container">
  <br>
  <div *ngIf="!device">
    <h3 class="text-center">Loading!</h3>
  </div>
  <div class="row" *ngIf="lastRecord">
    <div class="col-md-12">
      <div class="panel panel-info">
        <div class="panel-heading">
          <h3 class="panel-title">
                    {{device.name}}
              </h3>
          <span class="pull-right btn-click">
                  <i class="fa fa-chevron-circle-up"></i>
              </span>
        </div>
        <div class="clearfix"></div>
        <div class="table-responsive">
          <table class="table table-striped">
            <tr *ngIf="lastRecord">
              <td>X-Axis</td>
              <td>{{lastRecord.data.acclVals.x}}
{{lastRecord.data.acclVals.units}}</td>
            </tr>
            <tr *ngIf="lastRecord">
```

```
            <td>Y-Axis</td>
            <td>{{lastRecord.data.acclVals.y}}
{{lastRecord.data.acclVals.units}}</td>
          </tr>
          <tr *ngIf="lastRecord">
            <td>Z-Axis</td>
            <td>{{lastRecord.data.acclVals.z}}
{{lastRecord.data.acclVals.units}}</td>
          </tr>
          <tr *ngIf="lastRecord">
            <td>Signal Magnitude Vector</td>
            <td>{{lastRecord.data.acclVals.smv}}</td>
          </tr>
          <tr *ngIf="lastRecord">
            <td>Fall State</td>
            <td>{{lastRecord.data.acclVals.fall ? 'Patient Down' : 'All
is well!'}}</td>
          </tr>
          <tr *ngIf="lastRecord">
            <td>Location</td>
            <td>{{lastRecord.data.location.city}},
{{lastRecord.data.location.region}},
{{lastRecord.data.location.country}}</td>
          </tr>
          <tr *ngIf="lastRecord">
            <td>Received At</td>
            <td>{{lastRecord.createdAt | date : 'medium'}}</td>
          </tr>
        </table>
        <hr>
        <div class="col-md-12" *ngIf="acclVals.length > 0">
          <canvas baseChart [datasets]="acclVals"
[labels]="lineChartLabels" [options]="lineChartOptions"
[legend]="lineChartLegend" [chartType]="lineChartType"></canvas>
        </div>
      </div>
    </div>
  </div>
 </div>
</div>
```

Save the file and run:

```
npm start
```

We should see the following once we navigate to the device page:

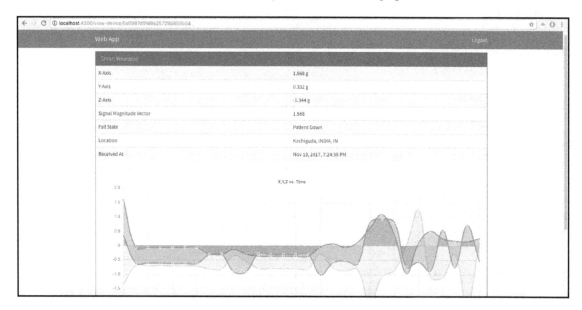

In the next section, we will update the desktop app.

Updating the desktop app

Now that the web app is done, we are going to build the same and deploy it inside our desktop app.

To get started, head back to the terminal/prompt of the web-app folder and run:

```
ng build --env=prod
```

This will create a new folder inside the `web-app` folder named `dist`. The contents of the `dist` folder should be along the lines of:

```
.
├── favicon.ico
├── index.html
├── inline.bundle.js
├── inline.bundle.js.map
├── main.bundle.js
├── main.bundle.js.map
├── polyfills.bundle.js
├── polyfills.bundle.js.map
├── scripts.bundle.js
├── scripts.bundle.js.map
├── styles.bundle.js
├── styles.bundle.js.map
├── vendor.bundle.js
└── vendor.bundle.js.map
```

All the code we have written is finally bundled into the preceding files. We will grab all of the files (not the `dist` folder) present inside the `dist` folder and then paste them inside the `desktop-app/app` folder. The final structure of the desktop app after these changes will be as follows:

```
.
├── app
|   ├── favicon.ico
|   ├── index.html
|   ├── inline.bundle.js
```

```
|   ├──── inline.bundle.js.map
|   ├──── main.bundle.js
|   ├──── main.bundle.js.map
|   ├──── polyfills.bundle.js
|   ├──── polyfills.bundle.js.map
|   ├──── scripts.bundle.js
|   ├──── scripts.bundle.js.map
|   ├──── styles.bundle.js
|   ├──── styles.bundle.js.map
|   ├──── vendor.bundle.js
|   └──── vendor.bundle.js.map
├──── freeport.js
├──── index.css
├──── index.html
├──── index.js
├──── license
├──── package.json
├──── readme.md
└──── server.js
```

To test drive, run:

```
npm start
```

Then, when we navigate to the **VIEW DEVICE** page, we should see the following:

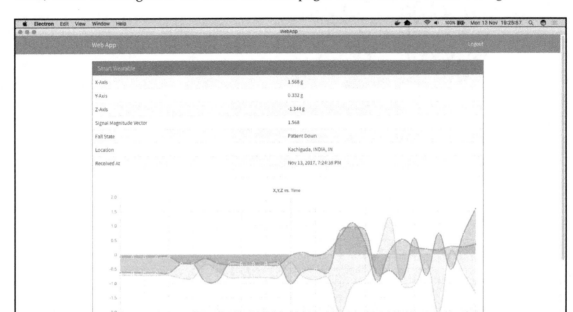

Now that we are done with the desktop app, we will work on the mobile app.

Updating the mobile app

To reflect the new template in the mobile app, we will update `mobile-app/src/pages/view-device/view-device.html`, as follows:

```
<ion-header>
  <ion-navbar>
    <ion-title>Mobile App</ion-title>
  </ion-navbar>
</ion-header>
<ion-content padding>
  <div *ngIf="!lastRecord">
    <h3 class="text-center">Loading!</h3>
  </div>
  <div *ngIf="lastRecord">
    <ion-list>
      <ion-item>
        <ion-label>Name</ion-label>
        <ion-label>{{device.name}}</ion-label>
```

```
        </ion-item>
        <ion-item>
          <ion-label>X-Axis</ion-label>
          <ion-label>{{lastRecord.data.acclVals.x}}
{{lastRecord.data.acclVals.units}}</ion-label>
        </ion-item>
        <ion-item>
          <ion-label>Y-Axis</ion-label>
          <ion-label>{{lastRecord.data.acclVals.y}}
{{lastRecord.data.acclVals.units}}</ion-label>
        </ion-item>
        <ion-item>
          <ion-label>Z-Axis</ion-label>
          <ion-label>{{lastRecord.data.acclVals.z}}
{{lastRecord.data.acclVals.units}}</ion-label>
        </ion-item>
        <ion-item>
          <ion-label>Signal Magnitude Vector</ion-label>
          <ion-label>{{lastRecord.data.acclVals.smv}}</ion-label>
        </ion-item>
        <ion-item>
          <ion-label>Fall State</ion-label>
          <ion-label>{{lastRecord.data.acclVals.fall ? 'Patient Down' : 'All
is well!'}}</ion-label>
        </ion-item>
        <ion-item>
          <ion-label>Location</ion-label>
          <ion-label>{{lastRecord.data.location.city}},
{{lastRecord.data.location.region}},
{{lastRecord.data.location.country}}</ion-label>
        </ion-item>
        <ion-item>
          <ion-label>Received At</ion-label>
          <ion-label>{{lastRecord.createdAt | date: 'medium'}}</ion-label>
        </ion-item>
      </ion-list>
    </div>
</ion-content>
```

Save all of the files and run the mobile app by using:

```
ionic serve
```

You could also use:

```
ionic cordova run android
```

We should see the following:

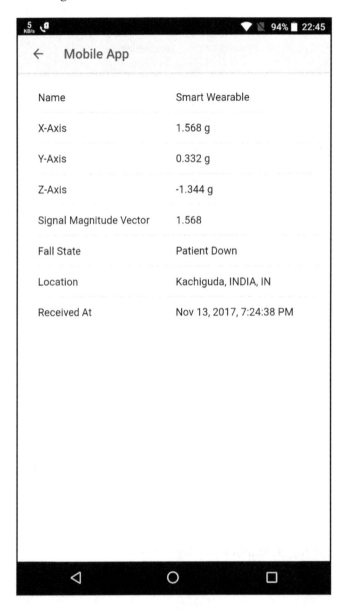

Summary

In this chapter, we worked with the concept of fall detection and IFTTT. Using the smart wearable we built in Chapter 6, *Smart Wearable*, we added the fall detection logic. Then, we posted the same data to the API engine, and in the API engine, we built our own IFTTT rules engine. We defined one rule for sending an email when a fall was detected.

As well as this, we also updated the web, desktop, and mobile apps to reflect the new data we collected.

In Chapter 8, *Raspberry Pi Image Streaming*, we are going to work with video surveillance using Raspberry Pi.

8

Raspberry Pi Image Streaming

In this chapter, we are going to look at live video streaming with Raspberry Pi 3 and Raspberry Pi camera. We are going to stream live video from Raspberry Pi 3 to our web browser and access this feed from anywhere in the world. As a next step, we are going to add a motion detector to the current setup and if the motion is detected, we then start streaming the video. In this chapter, we will go through the following topics:

- Understanding MJPEGs
- Setting up Raspberry Pi with Raspberry Pi camera
- Stream the images from the camera to the dashboard in real time
- Capturing video in motion

MJPEG

Quoting from Wikipedia, `https://en.wikipedia.org/wiki/Motion_JPEG`.

> *In multimedia, Motion JPEG (M-JPEG or MJPEG) is a video compression format in which each video frame or interlaced field of a digital video sequence is compressed separately as a JPEG image. Originally developed for multimedia PC applications, M-JPEG is now used by video-capture devices such as digital cameras, IP cameras, and webcams, as well as by non-linear video editing systems. It is natively supported by the QuickTime Player, the PlayStation console, and web browsers such as Safari, Google Chrome, Mozilla Firefox and Microsoft Edge.*

As described previously, we are going to capture a series of images, every `100ms` apart and stream the image binary data on a topic to the API engine, where we override an existing image with the latest image.

This streaming system is very simple and old-fashioned. There are no rewinds or pauses while streaming. We can always see the last frame.

Now that we have a high level of understanding of what we are going to achieve, let us get started.

Setting up Raspberry Pi

Raspberry Pi 3 set up with Raspberry Pi camera is quite simple. You can purchase a Raspberry Pi 3 camera (`https://www.raspberrypi.org/products/camera-module-v2/`) from any of the popular online vendors. Then you can follow this video to setup: camera board setup: `https://www.youtube.com/watch?v=GImeVqHQzsE`.

My camera setup is as follows:

I have used a stand and hoisted my camera on top of it.

Setting up the camera

Now that we have the camera connected and powered by the Raspberry Pi 3, we will set up the camera, as shown in the following steps:

1. From inside the Raspberry Pi, launch a new terminal and run:

   `sudo raspi-config`

2. This will launch the Raspberry Pi configuration screen. Select **Interfacing options**:

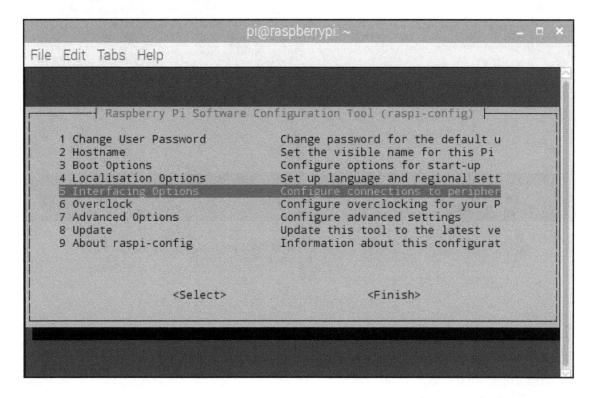

3. On the next screen, select **P1 Camera** and enable it:

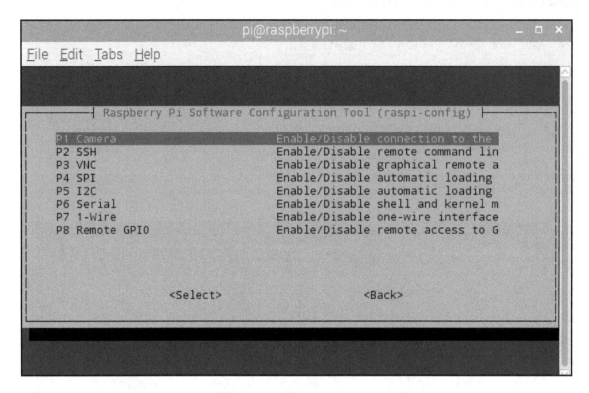

4. This will trigger a reboot, complete the reboot and log back into the Pi.

Once your camera is set up, we will test it.

Testing the camera

Now that the camera is set up and powered, let's test it. Open a new terminal and cd on the desktop. Then run the following:

```
raspistill -o test.jpg
```

This will take a screenshot in the present working directory, `Desktop`. The screen will look something like the following:

As you can see, `test.jpg` is created on the `Desktop` and when I double-click it shows a picture of the glass wall of my office.

Developing the logic

Now that we are able to test the camera, we will integrate this setup with our IoT platform. We are going to stream these images `100ms` apart continuously to our API engine and then through web sockets update the UI on the web.

To get started, we will make a copy of `chapter4` and dump it into a folder named `chapter8`. Inside the `chapter8` folder, open `pi/index.js` and update it as follows:

```
var config = require('./config.js');
var mqtt = require('mqtt');
var GetMac = require('getmac');
var Raspistill = require('node-raspistill').Raspistill;
var raspistill = new Raspistill({
```

```
        noFileSave: true,
        encoding: 'jpg',
        width: 640,
        height: 480
    });

    var crypto = require("crypto");
    var fs = require('fs');

    var client = mqtt.connect({
        port: config.mqtt.port,
        protocol: 'mqtts',
        host: config.mqtt.host,
        clientId: config.mqtt.clientId,
        reconnectPeriod: 1000,
        username: config.mqtt.clientId,
        password: config.mqtt.clientId,
        keepalive: 300,
        rejectUnauthorized: false
    });

    client.on('connect', function() {
        client.subscribe('rpi');
        GetMac.getMac(function(err, mac) {
            if (err) throw err;
            macAddress = mac;
            client.publish('api-engine', mac);
            startStreaming();
        });

    });

    client.on('message', function(topic, message) {
        message = message.toString();
        if (topic === 'rpi') {
            console.log('API Engine Response >> ', message);
        } else {
            console.log('Unknown topic', topic);
        }
    });

    function startStreaming() {
        raspistill
            .timelapse(100, 0, function(image) { // every 100ms ~~FOREVER~~
                var data2Send = {
                    data: {
                        image: image,
                        id: crypto.randomBytes(8).toString("hex")
```

```
        },
        macAddress: macAddress
    };

    client.publish('image', JSON.stringify(data2Send));
    console.log('[image]', 'published');
    })
    .then(function() {
        console.log('Timelapse Ended')
    })
    .catch(function(err) {
        console.log('Error', err);
    });
}
```

As we can see from the preceding code, we are waiting for the MQTT connection to be completed, once the connection is completed, we call `startStreaming()` to start streaming. Inside `startStreaming()`, we are calling `raspistill.timelapse()` passing in `100`ms, as time difference between each click and `0` indicates that the capture should continue perpetually.

Once the image is captured, we construct the `data2Send` object with a random ID, the image buffer, and the device `macAddress`. Before publishing to the image topic, we stringify the `data2Send` object.

Now, move this file to Raspberry Pi's `pi-client` folder, present on the desktop. And from inside Raspberry Pi's, `pi-client` folder, run:

```
npm install && npm install node-raspistill --save
```

These two commands will install the `node-raspistill` and other node modules present inside the `package.json` file.

With this, we are done with the setup of the Raspberry Pi and the camera. In the next section, we will update the API engine to accept the live streaming of images.

Updating the API engine

Now that we are done with the Raspberry Pi setup, we will update the API engine to accept the incoming data.

The first thing we are going to do is update `api-engine/server/mqtt/index.js` as follows:

```javascript
var Data = require('../api/data/data.model');
var mqtt = require('mqtt');
var config = require('../config/environment');
var fs = require('fs');
var client = mqtt.connect({
    port: config.mqtt.port,
    protocol: 'mqtts',
    host: config.mqtt.host,
    clientId: config.mqtt.clientId,
    reconnectPeriod: 1000,
    username: config.mqtt.clientId,
    password: config.mqtt.clientId,
    keepalive: 300,
    rejectUnauthorized: false
});

client.on('connect', function() {
    console.log('Connected to Mosca at ' + config.mqtt.host + ' on port ' +
config.mqtt.port);
    client.subscribe('api-engine');
    client.subscribe('image');
});

client.on('message', function(topic, message) {
    // message is Buffer
    // console.log('Topic >> ', topic);
    // console.log('Message >> ', message.toString());
    if (topic === 'api-engine') {
        var macAddress = message.toString();
        console.log('Mac Address >> ', macAddress);
        client.publish('rpi', 'Got Mac Address: ' + macAddress);
    } else if (topic === 'image') {
        message = JSON.parse(message.toString());
        // convert string to buffer
        var image = Buffer.from(message.data.image, 'utf8');
        var fname = 'stream_' + ((message.macAddress).replace(/:/g, '_')) +
'.jpg';
        fs.writeFile(__dirname + '/stream/' + fname, image, { encoding:
'binary' }, function(err) {
            if (err) {
                console.log('[image]', 'save failed', err);
            } else {
                console.log('[image]', 'saved');
            }
```

```
    });

    // as of now we are not going to
    // store the image buffer in DB.
    // Gridfs would be a good way
    // instead of storing a stringified text
    delete message.data.image;
    message.data.fname = fname;

    // create a new data record for the device
    Data.create(message, function(err, data) {
        if (err) return console.error(err);
        // if the record has been saved successfully,
        // websockets will trigger a message to the web-app
        // console.log('Data Saved :', data);
    });
    } else {
        console.log('Unknown topic', topic);
    }
});
```

As we can see from the preceding code, inside the message event of MQTT, we have added a new topic named `image`. Inside this topic, we extract the string format of the image buffer and convert it back to the image binary data. Then using the `fs` module, we overwrite the same image again and again.

We also keep saving the data simultaneously to MongoDB and this will trigger a socket emit.

As the next step, we need to create a folder named `stream` inside the `mqtt` folder. And inside this folder, drop an image present here: `http://www.iconarchive.com/show/small-n-flat-icons-by-paomedia/sign-ban -icon.html`. This image will be shown if there is no feed available for a camera.

All the images will be saved inside the `stream` folder and the same image will be updated for the same device, as mentioned earlier, there will not be any rewinds or replays.

Now, the images get saved inside the `stream` folder and we need to expose an end point to send this image to the request clients. For that, open `api-engine/server/routes.js` and add the following to the `module.exports` function:

```
app.get('/stream/:fname', function(req, res, next) {
        var fname = req.params.fname;
        var streamDir = __dirname + '/mqtt/stream/';
        var img = streamDir + fname;
        console.log(img);
```

```
            fs.exists(img, function(exists) {
          if (exists) {
                   return res.sendFile(img);
              } else {
                   //
  http://www.iconarchive.com/show/small-n-flat-icons-by-paomedia/sign-ban-ico
  n.html
                   return res.sendFile(streamDir + '/no-image.png');
              }
          });
      });
```

This will take care of dispatching the image to the client (web, desktop, and mobile).

With this, we are done with setting up the API engine.

Save all the files and start the broker, API engine, and the `pi-client`. If everything is successfully set up, we should see the data being posted from the Raspberry Pi:

And the same data appearing in the API engine:

```
● ● ●          api-engine — npm start — node · npm TERM_PROGRAM=Apple_Terminal SHELL=/bin/zsh — 107×25
        mosca    node /usr/local...                    npm    node · npm T...       npm                    +
[nodemon] to restart at any time, enter `rs`
[nodemon] watching: *.*
[nodemon] starting `node server/app.js`
Express server listening on 9000, in development mode
Connected to Mosca at 127.0.0.1 on port 8883
Mac Address >>  b8:27:eb:39:92:0d
[image] saved
[image] saved
[image] saved
[image] saved
[image] saved
[image] saved
[image] saved
[image] saved
[image] saved
[image] saved
[image] saved
[image] saved
[image] saved
[image] saved
[image] saved
[image] saved
[image] saved
[image] saved
```

At this point, the images are being captured and sent to the API engine over MQTTs. The next step is to view these images in real time.

Updating the web app

Now that the data is streaming to the API engine, we will show it on the web app. Open `web-app/src/app/device/device.component.html` and update it as follows:

```html
<div class="container">
    <br>
    <div *ngIf="!device">
        <h3 class="text-center">Loading!</h3>
    </div>
    <div class="row" *ngIf="!lastRecord">
        <h3 class="text-center">No Data!</h3>
    </div>
    <div class="row" *ngIf="lastRecord">
        <div class="col-md-12">
            <div class="panel panel-info">
                <div class="panel-heading">
                    <h3 class="panel-title">
```

```
                        {{device.name}}
                    </h3>
                    <span class="pull-right btn-click">
                        <i class="fa fa-chevron-circle-up"></i>
                    </span>
                </div>
                <div class="clearfix"></div>
                <div class="table-responsive" *ngIf="lastRecord">
                    <table class="table table-striped">
                        <tr>
                            <td colspan="2" class="text-center"><img
[src]="lastRecord.data.fname"></td>
                        </tr>
                        <tr class="text-center" >
                            <td>Received At</td>
                            <td>{{lastRecord.createdAt | date:
'medium'}}</td>
                        </tr>
                    </table>
                </div>
            </div>
        </div>
    </div>
</div>
```

Here, we are displaying the image that we have created in real time. Next, update web-app/src/app/device/device.component.ts as follows:

```
import { Component, OnInit, OnDestroy } from '@angular/core';
import { DevicesService } from '../services/devices.service';
import { Params, ActivatedRoute } from '@angular/router';
import { SocketService } from '../services/socket.service';
import { DataService } from '../services/data.service';
import { NotificationsService } from 'angular2-notifications';
import { Globals } from '../app.global';

@Component({
    selector: 'app-device',
    templateUrl: './device.component.html',
    styleUrls: ['./device.component.css']
})
export class DeviceComponent implements OnInit, OnDestroy {
    device: any;
    data: Array<any>;
    toggleState: boolean = false;
    private subDevice: any;
    private subData: any;
```

```
    lastRecord: any;

    // line chart config

    constructor(private deviceService: DevicesService,
          private socketService: SocketService,
          private dataService: DataService,
          private route: ActivatedRoute,
          private notificationsService: NotificationsService) { }

    ngOnInit() {
          this.subDevice = this.route.params.subscribe((params) => {
                this.deviceService.getOne(params['id']).subscribe((response)
=> {
                      this.device = response.json();
                      this.getData();
                });
          });
    }

    getData() {
          this.dataService.get(this.device.macAddress).subscribe((response)
=> {
                this.data = response.json();
                let d = this.data[0];
                d.data.fname = Globals.BASE_API_URL + 'stream/' +
d.data.fname;
                this.lastRecord = d; // descending order data
                this.socketInit();
          });
    }

    socketInit() {
          this.subData =
this.socketService.getData(this.device.macAddress).subscribe((data: any) =>
{
                if (this.data.length <= 0) return;
                this.data.splice(this.data.length - 1, 1); // remove the
last record
                data.data.fname = Globals.BASE_API_URL + 'stream/' +
data.data.fname + '?t=' + (Math.random() * 100000); // cache busting
                this.data.push(data); // add the new one
                this.lastRecord = data;
          });
    }
```

```
ngOnDestroy() {
    this.subDevice.unsubscribe();
    this.subData ? this.subData.unsubscribe() : '';
}
}
```

Here we are constructing the image URL and pointing it to the API engine. Save all the files and launch the web app by running the following command from inside the `web-app` folder:

```
npm start
```

If everything works as expected, upon navigating to the **VIEW DEVICE** page, we should see the video stream very slowly. I am monitoring a cup placed in front of my chair as follows:

Updating the desktop app

Now that the web app is done, we are going to build the same and deploy it inside our desktop app.

To get started, head back to the terminal/prompt of the web-app folder and run the following:

```
ng build --env=prod
```

This will create a new folder inside the web-app folder named dist. The contents of the dist folder should be along the lines of:

```
├──── favicon.ico

├──── index.html

├──── inline.bundle.js

├──── inline.bundle.js.map

├──── main.bundle.js

├──── main.bundle.js.map

├──── polyfills.bundle.js

├──── polyfills.bundle.js.map

├──── scripts.bundle.js

├──── scripts.bundle.js.map

├──── styles.bundle.js

├──── styles.bundle.js.map

├──── vendor.bundle.js

└──── vendor.bundle.js.map
```

All the code we have written is finally bundled into the preceding files. We will grab all the files (not the `dist` folder) present inside the `dist` folder and then paste it inside the `desktop-app/app` folder. The final structure of the `desktop-app` after the preceding changes will be as follows:

```
.
├── app
│   ├── favicon.ico
│   ├── index.html
│   ├── inline.bundle.js
│   ├── inline.bundle.js.map
│   ├── main.bundle.js
│   ├── main.bundle.js.map
│   ├── polyfills.bundle.js
│   ├── polyfills.bundle.js.map
│   ├── scripts.bundle.js
│   ├── scripts.bundle.js.map
│   ├── styles.bundle.js
│   ├── styles.bundle.js.map
│   ├── vendor.bundle.js
│   └── vendor.bundle.js.map
├── freeport.js
├── index.css
├── index.html
├── index.js
├── license
```

```
├── package.json
├── readme.md
└── server.js
```

To test drive, run the following:

npm start

And then when we navigate to the **VIEW DEVICE** page, we should see:

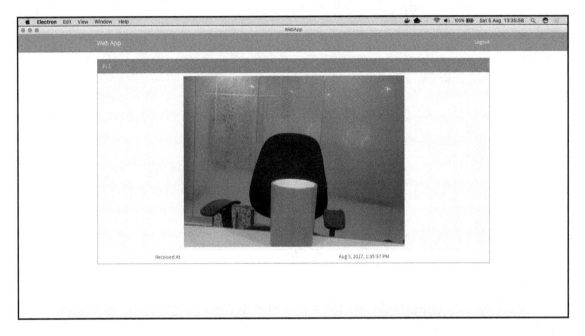

With this we are done with the development of the desktop app. In the next section, we will update the mobile app.

Updating the mobile app

In the last section, we have updated the desktop app. In this section, we are going to update the mobile app template to stream images.

First we are going to update the view-device template. Update `mobile-app/src/pages/view-device/view-device.html` as follows:

```html
<ion-header>
    <ion-navbar>
        <ion-title>Mobile App</ion-title>
    </ion-navbar>
</ion-header>
<ion-content padding>
    <div *ngIf="!lastRecord">
        <h3 class="text-center">Loading!</h3>
    </div>
    <div *ngIf="lastRecord">
        <ion-list>
            <ion-item>
                <img [src]="lastRecord.data.fname">
            </ion-item>
            <ion-item>
                <ion-label>Received At</ion-label>
                <ion-label>{{lastRecord.createdAt | date: 'medium'}}</ion-
label>
            </ion-item>
        </ion-list>
    </div>
</ion-content>
```

The logic for displaying the image stream on a mobile is the same as web/desktop. Next, update `mobile-app/src/pages/view-device/view-device.ts` as follows:

```typescript
import { Component } from '@angular/core';
import { IonicPage, NavController, NavParams } from 'ionic-angular';
import { Globals } from '../../app/app.globals';
import { DevicesService } from '../../services/device.service';
import { DataService } from '../../services/data.service';
import { ToastService } from '../../services/toast.service';
import { SocketService } from '../../services/socket.service';

@IonicPage()
@Component({
    selector: 'page-view-device',
    templateUrl: 'view-device.html',
})
```

```
export class ViewDevicePage {
    device: any;
    data: Array<any>;
    toggleState: boolean = false;
    private subData: any;
    lastRecord: any;


    constructor(private navCtrl: NavController,
            private navParams: NavParams,
            private socketService: SocketService,
            private deviceService: DevicesService,
            private dataService: DataService,
            private toastService: ToastService) {
            this.device = navParams.get("device");
            console.log(this.device);
    }

    ionViewDidLoad() {
            this.deviceService.getOne(this.device._id).subscribe((response) =>
{
                    this.device = response.json();
                    this.getData();
            });
    }

    getData() {
            this.dataService.get(this.device.macAddress).subscribe((response)
=> {
                    this.data = response.json();
                    let d = this.data[0];
                    d.data.fname = Globals.BASE_API_URL + 'stream/' +
d.data.fname;
                    this.lastRecord = d; // descending order data
                    this.socketInit();
            });
    }

    socketInit() {
            this.subData =
this.socketService.getData(this.device.macAddress).subscribe((data: any) =>
{
                    if(this.data.length <= 0) return;
                    this.data.splice(this.data.length - 1, 1); // remove the
last record
                    data.data.fname = Globals.BASE_API_URL + 'stream/' +
data.data.fname + '?t=' + (Math.random() * 100000);
                    this.data.push(data); // add the new one
```

```
            this.lastRecord = data;
        });
    }

    ionViewDidUnload() {
        this.subData && this.subData.unsubscribe &&
    this.subData.unsubscribe(); //unsubscribe if subData is defined
    }
}
```

Save all the files and run the mobile app either by using:

ionic serve

Or by using the following code:

ionic cordova run android

And we should see the following:

With this we are done with displaying the data from the camera on the mobile app.

Motion-based video capture

As we could see that the stream was kind of choppy, slow, and not real time, another probable solution is to put a motion detector along with our Raspberry Pi and camera. Then when a motion is identified, we start taking a video for 10 seconds. Then we email this video to the user as an attachment.

Now, we will start updating our existing code.

Updating the Raspberry Pi

To get started, we will update our Raspberry Pi setup to accommodate an HC-SR501 PIR sensor. You can find a PIR sensor here: `https://www.amazon.com/Motion-HC-SR501-Infrared-Arduino-Raspberry/dp/B00M1H7KBW/ref=sr_1_4_a_it`.

We will connect the PIR sensor to the Raspberry Pi on pin 17 and the camera to the camera slot as we have seen earlier.

Once the connections are made as previously discussed, update `pi/index.js` as follows:

```
var config = require('./config.js');
var mqtt = require('mqtt');
var GetMac = require('getmac');
var Raspistill = require('node-raspistill').Raspistill;
var crypto = require("crypto");
var fs = require('fs');
var Gpio = require('onoff').Gpio;
var exec = require('child_process').exec;

var pir = new Gpio(17, 'in', 'both');
var raspistill = new Raspistill({
    noFileSave: true,
    encoding: 'jpg',
    width: 640,
    height: 480
});

var client = mqtt.connect({
    port: config.mqtt.port,
    protocol: 'mqtts',
```

```
    host: config.mqtt.host,
    clientId: config.mqtt.clientId,
    reconnectPeriod: 1000,
    username: config.mqtt.clientId,
    password: config.mqtt.clientId,
    keepalive: 300,
    rejectUnauthorized: false
});

client.on('connect', function() {
    client.subscribe('rpi');
    GetMac.getMac(function(err, mac) {
        if (err) throw err;
        macAddress = mac;
        client.publish('api-engine', mac);
        // startStreaming();
    });

});

client.on('message', function(topic, message) {
    message = message.toString();
    if (topic === 'rpi') {
        console.log('API Engine Response >> ', message);
    } else {
        console.log('Unknown topic', topic);
    }
});

function startStreaming() {
    raspistill
        .timelapse(100, 0, function(image) { // every 100ms ~~FOREVER~~
            var data2Send = {
                data: {
                    image: image,
                    id: crypto.randomBytes(8).toString("hex")
                },
                macAddress: macAddress
            };

            client.publish('image', JSON.stringify(data2Send));
            console.log('[image]', 'published');
        })
        .then(function() {
            console.log('Timelapse Ended')
        })
        .catch(function(err) {
            console.log('Error', err);
```

```
        });
    }

var isRec = false;

// keep watching for motion
pir.watch(function(err, value) {
    if (err) exit();
    if (value == 1 && !isRec) {
        console.log('Intruder detected');
        console.log('capturing video.. ');
        isRec = true;
        var videoPath = __dirname + '/video.h264';
        var file = fs.createWriteStream(videoPath);
        var video_path = './video/video' + Date.now() + '.h264';
        var cmd = 'raspivid -o ' + video_path + ' -t 5000';

        exec(cmd, function(error, stdout, stderr) {
            // output is in stdout
            console.log('Video Saved @ : ', video_path);
            require('./mailer').sendEmail(video_path, true, function(err,
info) {
                setTimeout(function() {
                    // isRec = false;
                }, 3000); // don't allow recording for 3 sec after
            });
        });
    }
});

function exit() {
    pir.unexport();
    process.exit();
}
```

As we can see from the preceding code, we have marked GPIO 17 as an input pin and assigned it to a variable named `pir`. Next, using `pir.watch()`, we keep looking for a change in value on the motion detector. If the motion detector has detected some change, we will check if the value is 1, which indicates that a motion is triggered. Then using `raspivid` we record a 5 second video and email it.

For the logic needed to send an email from Raspberry Pi 3, create a new file named `mailer.js` at the root of the `pi-client` folder and update it as follows:

```
var fs = require('fs');
var nodemailer = require('nodemailer');
```

```
var transporter = nodemailer.createTransport({
    service: 'Gmail',
    auth: {
        user: 'arvind.ravulavaru@gmail.com',
        pass: '**********'
    }
});

var timerId;

module.exports.sendEmail = function(file, deleteAfterUpload, cb) {
    if (timerId) return;

    timerId = setTimeout(function() {
        clearTimeout(timerId);
        timerId = null;
    }, 10000);

    console.log('Sendig an Email..');

    var mailOptions = {
        from: 'Pi Bot <pi.intruder.alert@gmail.com>',
        to: 'user@email.com',
        subject: '[Pi Bot] Intruder Detected',
        html: 'Intruder Detected. Please check the video attached.
<br/><br/> Intruder Detected At : ' + Date(),
        attachments: [{
            path: file
        }]
    };

    transporter.sendMail(mailOptions, function(err, info) {
        if (err) {
            console.log(err);
        } else {
            console.log('Message sent: ' + info.response);
            if (deleteAfterUpload) {
                fs.unlink(path);
            }
        }

        if (cb) {
            cb(err, info);
        }
    });
}
```

We are using nodemailer to send an email. Update the credentials as applicable.

Next, run the following command:

```
npm install onoff -save
```

In the next section, we are going to test this setup.

Testing the code

Now that we are done with the setup, let us test it. Power Raspberry Pi, upload the code if not done already, and run the following:

```
npm start
```

Once the code is running, trigger a motion. This will start the camera recording and save the video for five seconds. Then this video will be emailed to the user. The following is a list of the output:

The received email would be as follows:

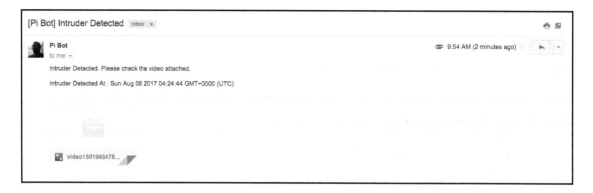

This is an alternative of using Raspberry Pi 3 for surveillance.

Summary

In this chapter, we have seen two methods of surveillance using Raspberry Pi. The first approach is where we have streamed images to the API engine and then visualized the same on the mobile web and desktop applications using MJPEG. The second approach is to detect a motion and then start recording a video. Then email this video as an attachment. The two approaches can be combined together as well and the MJPEG streaming can be started if a motion is detected in approach one.

In Chapter 9, *Smart Surveillance*, we are going to take this to the next level, we are going to add face recognition on top of our captures and perform face recognition (not face detection) using the AWS Rekognition platform.

9
Smart Surveillance

In Chapter 8, *Raspberry Pi Image Streaming*, we learned how to connect a Raspberry Pi camera module to Raspberry Pi 3, grab a picture or video, and then upload/stream it in real time. In this chapter, we are going to take this logic to the next level. We are going to take a picture when there is an intrusion detected, and then send that image to the Amazon Rekognition platform and compare the image against a set of images.

In this chapter, we are going to cover the following points:

- Understanding AWS Rekognition
- Seeding an AWS Rekognition collection with authorized faces
- Taking pictures from Raspberry Pi 3 upon intrusion and comparing them with the seed faces

AWS Rekognition

The following quote is from Amazon Rekognition (https://aws.amazon.com/rekognition/):

> *"Amazon Rekognition is a service that makes it easy to add image analysis to your applications. With Rekognition, you can detect objects, scenes, faces; recognize celebrities; and identify inappropriate content in images. You can also search and compare faces. Rekognition's API enables you to quickly add sophisticated deep learning-based visual search and image classification to your applications."*

In this chapter, we are going to leverage the AWS Rekognition feature to help us set conditional surveillance based on face recognition, not face detection.

Let's say that you had set up a camera at your house entrance using Raspberry Pi, and programmed it to keep taking pictures of intruders and sending them to you. In this setup, you will be receiving images of everyone who comes to your door, for instance, your family, neighbors, and so on. But what if you are notified only if the intruder is an unknown person? Now, that is what I call smart surveillance.

In `Chapter 8`, *Raspberry Pi Image Streaming*, we built a setup that captured images when intrusion is detected and which then send an email and updated the apps in real time.

In this chapter, we are going seed AWS Rekognition with a set of faces that are trusted. Then, when there is an image captured by the camera, upon intrusion detection, we send it to AWS Rekognition to perform facial recognition. If the image matches one of the trusted images, nothing happens; otherwise, an email notification is sent.

To understand more about AWS Rekogniton and how it works, take a look at *Announcing Amazon Rekognition - Deep Learning-Based Image Analysis* (`https://www.youtube.com/watch?v=b6gN9jCmq3w`).

Setting up smart surveillance

Now that we have an understanding of what we are going to do, we will get started with the setup of Raspberry Pi.

We are going to set up the camera and a motion detector, as we did in `Chapter 8`, *Raspberry Pi Image Streaming*. Next, we will be adding the logic required to capture an image upon the detection of motion and then send it for processing.

Before we do that, we need to seed the Rekognition collection with authorized faces.

This script can be an API as part of the API engine, and using the web dashboard we can upload and seed the images. But to keep things simple, we are going to run this standalone script from a machine.

Setting up AWS credentials

Before we get started with development, we need to set up our local machine with the AWS CLI and AWS credentials.

First, we need to install the AWS CLI. Head over to `https://aws.amazon.com/cli` and follow the instructions on the page. To test the installation from the command prompt, run:

```
aws --version
```

You should see something like:

```
aws-cli/1.7.38 Python/2.7.9 Darwin/16.1.0
```

Once the setup is complete we need to configure the AWS credentials, so that as long as we are using this machine, we need not enter any credentials within the code.

Run the following:

```
aws configure
```

You should be presented with four questions; fill them with the appropriate information:

```
→  ~ aws configure
AWS Access Key ID [****************KWNA]: ****************************
AWS Secret Access Key [****************io/6]: **************************
Default region name [ap-southeast-1]: ap-southeast-1
Default output format [None]: json
```

If you are facing issues when configuring AWS credentials, refer to `http://docs.aws.amazon.com/cli/latest/userguide/cli-chap-getting-started.html#cli-quick-configuration`.

Another option is to add the `accessKeyId` and `secretAccessKey` in the code itself. But we would still need the `accessKeyId` and `secretAccessKey` to continue.

Once the configuration is done, we will get started interfacing with AWS Rekognition.

Seeding the authorized faces

Create a folder named `chapter9`, and inside this folder, create a folder named `rekogniton_seed`. Inside this folder, create a file named `seed.js`.

Update `seed.js` as follows:

```
var config = {
    collectionName: 'AIOWJS-FACES',
    region: 'eu-west-1',
// If the credentials are set using `aws configure`, below two properties
are not needed.
    accessKeyId: 'YOUR-ACCESSKEYID',
    secretAccessKey: YOUR-SECRETACCESSKEY'
};

var AWS = require('aws-sdk');
var fs = require('fs-extra');
var path = require('path');
var klawSync = require('klaw-sync')
AWS.config.region = config.region;

var rekognition = new AWS.Rekognition({
    region: config.region,
 // accessKeyId: config.accessKeyId, // uncomment as applicable
 // secretAccessKey: config.secretAccessKey // uncomment as applicable
});

function createCollection() {
    rekognition.createCollection({
        'CollectionId': config.collectionName
    }, (err, data) => {
        if (err) {
            console.log(err, err.stack); // an error occurred
        } else {
            console.log(data); // successful response
        }
    });
}

function indexFaces() {
    var paths = klawSync('./faces', {
        nodir: true,
        ignore: ['*.json']
    });

    paths.forEach((file) => {
        var p = path.parse(file.path);
        var name = p.name.replace(/\W/g, '');
        var bitmap = fs.readFileSync(file.path);

        rekognition.indexFaces({
```

```
                   'CollectionId': config.collectionName,
                   'DetectionAttributes': ['ALL'],
                   'ExternalImageId': name,
                   'Image': {
                       'Bytes': bitmap
                   }
              }, (err, data) => {
                   if (err) {
                       console.log(err, err.stack); // an error occurred
                   } else {
                       console.log(data.FaceRecords); // successful response
                       fs.writeJson(file.path + '.json', data, (err) => {
                           if (err) return console.error(err)
                       });
                   }
              });
         });
    }

    createCollection();
    indexFaces();
```

Please refer to the source code for the additional comments: `https://github.com/PacktPublishing/Practical-Internet-of-Things-with-JavaScript`.

As we see from the preceding code snippet, we are creating a new collection named AIOWJS-FACES in the eu-west-1 region. You can either use the accessKeyId and secretAccessKey from within the code, or you can use the ones from AWS CLI configure. If you are using the key and secret from AWS CLI configure, you can comment these two lines out while initializing a new instance of rekognition.

We call the createCollection() to create a new collection and this needs to be run only once.

You can seed data as many times as you want, but collection creation should happen only once.

Once the collection is created, we will index a few images from a folder named faces, which we will create now. Create a folder named faces at the root of the rekogniton_seed folder. Inside this folder, upload clear images with faces. The better the quality and clarity of the image is, the better chance it has of being recognized.

I have dumped a couple of pictures of mine inside the `faces` folder. Before we start the seeding, we need to install the required dependencies:

1. Open command prompt/terminal inside the `rekogniton_seed` folder and run:

   npm init --yes

2. Next, run:

   npm install aws-sdk fs-extra klaw-sync --save

3. Once the installation is complete, create the collection and seed the faces by running:

   node seed.js

4. We should see an output something like the following for each uploaded image:

```
[ { Face:
    { FaceId: '2d7ac2b3-fa84-5a16-ad8c-7fa670b8ec8c',
      BoundingBox: [Object],
      ImageId: '61a299b6-3004-576d-b966-31fb6780f1c7',
      ExternalImageId: 'photo',
      Confidence: 99.96211242675781 },
  FaceDetail:
    { BoundingBox: [Object],
      AgeRange: [Object],
      Smile: [Object],
      Eyeglasses: [Object],
      Sunglasses: [Object],
      Gender: [Object],
      Beard: [Object],
      Mustache: [Object],
      EyesOpen: [Object],
      MouthOpen: [Object],
      Emotions: [Object],
      Landmarks: [Object],
      Pose: [Object],
      Quality: [Object],
      Confidence: 99.96211242675781 } } ]
```

This object will consist of information about the image that was analyzed by Rekognition.

You can look up the *.json files inside the faces folder once the seeding is complete. These JSON files will consist of more information about the image.

Testing the seed

Now that the seed is completed, let's validate the seed. This step is totally optional; you can skip this step if you want to.

Create a new folder named rekogniton_seed_test at the root of the chapter9 folder. Then create a folder named faces at the root of rekogniton_seed_test and dump the image that you would like to test into this folder. In my case, the picture is of me at a different location.

Next, create a file named seed_test.js and update it, as shown here:

```
var config = {
    collectionName: 'AIOWJS-FACES',
    region: 'eu-west-1',
    accessKeyId: 'ACCESSKEYID',
    secretAccessKey: SECRETACCESSKEY'
};

var AWS = require('aws-sdk');
var fs = require('fs-extra');
var path = require('path');
var klawSync = require('klaw-sync')
AWS.config.region = config.region;

var rekognition = new AWS.Rekognition({
    region: config.region,
    // accessKeyId: config.accessKeyId, // uncomment as applicable
    // secretAccessKey: config.secretAccessKey // uncomment as applicable
});


// Once you've created your collection you can run this to test it out.
function FaceSearchTest(imagePath) {
    var bitmap = fs.readFileSync(imagePath);

    rekognition.searchFacesByImage({
        "CollectionId": config.collectionName,
        "FaceMatchThreshold": 80,
        "Image": {
            "Bytes": bitmap,
        },
```

```
        "MaxFaces": 1
    }, (err, data) => {
        if (err) {
            console.error(err, err.stack); // an error occurred
        } else {
            // console.log(data); // successful response
            console.log(data.FaceMatches.length > 0 ?
data.FaceMatches[0].Face : data);
        }
    });
}


FaceSearchTest(__dirname + '/faces/arvind_2.jpg');
```

In the preceding code, we pick up the image from the `faces` folder and submit it for recognition, and then we print the appropriate response.

Once that is done, we will install the required dependencies:

1. Open command prompt/terminal inside the `rekogniton_seed_test` folder and run:

   npm init --yes

2. Then run:

   npm install aws-sdk fs-extra path --save

3. Now, we are all set to run this example. From inside the `rekogniton_seed_test` folder, run:

   node seed_test.js

4. We should see something like the following:

   ```
   { FaceId: '2d7ac2b3-fa84-5a16-ad8c-7fa670b8ec8c',
     BoundingBox:
      { Width: 0.4594019949436188,
        Height: 0.4594019949436188,
        Left: 0.3076919913291931,
        Top: 0.2820509970188141 },
     ImageId: '61a299b6-3004-576d-b966-31fb6780f1c7',
     ExternalImageId: 'photo',
     Confidence: 99.96209716796875 }
   ```

There are a couple of things to note from the preceding response:

- `FaceId`: This is the ID against which the current face has been matched
- `ImageId`: This is the image against which the current face has been matched

With this, we can even tag users from the images that we have indexed/seeded.

You can do a negative test by putting an image that doesn't match our seed data and updating the last line in the preceding code as follows:

```
FaceSearchTest(__dirname + '/faces/no_arvind.jpg');
```

We should see something like the following:

```
{ SearchedFaceBoundingBox:

{ Width: 0.5322222113609314,

Height: 0.5333333611488342,

Left: 0.2777777910232544,

Top: 0.12444444745779037 },

SearchedFaceConfidence: 99.76634979248047,

FaceMatches: [] }
```

As you can see, there were no matches found.

We are going to use the preceding method in our Raspberry Pi, once we have captured an image.

Deploying to Raspberry Pi

Now that we have seeded a Rekognition collection, as well as tested it (an optional step), we are now going to start setting up the Raspberry Pi code.

We will be using all the other code pieces from the `chapter8` folder as is and only modifying the Raspberry Pi client in the `chapter9` folder.

Copy the entire code from the `chapter8` folder into the `chapter9` folder. Then, open the `pi-client` folder either on your desktop or on the Raspberry Pi itself, and update it as follows:

```
var config = require('./config.js');
var mqtt = require('mqtt');
var GetMac = require('getmac');
var Raspistill = require('node-raspistill').Raspistill;
var crypto = require("crypto");
var Gpio = require('onoff').Gpio;
var exec = require('child_process').exec;

var AWS = require('aws-sdk');

var pir = new Gpio(17, 'in', 'both');
var raspistill = new Raspistill({
    noFileSave: true,
    encoding: 'bmp',
    width: 640,
    height: 480
});

// Rekognition config
var config = {
    collectionName: 'AIOWJS-FACES',
    region: 'eu-west-1',
    accessKeyId: 'ACCESSKEYID',
    secretAccessKey: 'SECRETACCESSKEY'
};

AWS.config.region = config.region;

var rekognition = new AWS.Rekognition({
    region: config.region,
    accessKeyId: config.accessKeyId,
    secretAccessKey: config.secretAccessKey
});

var client = mqtt.connect({
    port: config.mqtt.port,
    protocol: 'mqtts',
    host: config.mqtt.host,
    clientId: config.mqtt.clientId,
    reconnectPeriod: 1000,
    username: config.mqtt.clientId,
    password: config.mqtt.clientId,
    keepalive: 300,
```

```
        rejectUnauthorized: false
});

client.on('connect', function() {
    client.subscribe('rpi');
    GetMac.getMac(function(err, mac) {
        if (err) throw err;
        macAddress = mac;
        client.publish('api-engine', mac);
        // startStreaming();
    });

});

client.on('message', function(topic, message) {
    message = message.toString();
    if (topic === 'rpi') {
        console.log('API Engine Response >> ', message);
    } else {
        console.log('Unknown topic', topic);
    }
});


var processing = false;

// keep watching for motion
pir.watch(function(err, value) {
    if (err) exit();
    if (value == 1 && !processing) {
        raspistill.takePhoto()
            .then((photo) => {
                console.log('took photo');
                checkForMatch(photo, function(err, authorizedFace) {
                    if (err) {
                        console.error(err);
                    } else {
                        if (authorizedFace) {
                            console.log('User Authorized');
                        } else {
                            // unauthorized user,
                            // send an email!
                            require('./mailer').sendEmail(photo,
function(err, info) {
                                if (err) {
                                    console.error(err);
                                } else {
                                    console.log('Email Send Success',
```

```
      info);
                                           }
                                       });
                               }
                           }
                       });
                   })
                   .catch((error) => {
                       console.error('something bad happened', error);
                   });
           }
       });

       function checkForMatch(image, cb) {
           rekognition.searchFacesByImage({
               'CollectionId': config.collectionName,
               'FaceMatchThreshold': 80,
               'Image': {
                   'Bytes': image,
               },
               'MaxFaces': 1
           }, (err, data) => {
               if (err) {
                   console.error(err, err.stack); // an error occurred
                   cb(err, null);
               } else {
                   // console.log(data); // successful response
                   console.log(data.FaceMatches.length > 0 ?
       data.FaceMatches[0].Face : data);
                   cb(null, data.FaceMatches.length >= 1);
               }
           });
       }

       function exit() {
           pir.unexport();
           process.exit();
       }
```

In the preceding code, we have the required configuration to make a request to AWS Rekognition, and then we run `checkForMatch()`, which will take the raw photo and check for matches. If any matches are found, we will not get an email, and if no matches are found, we will get an email.

Next, we will install the required dependencies.

Run the following:

```
npm install getmac mqtt node-raspistill aws-sdk --save
```

Once the installation is done, start the broker, `api-engine`, and web dashboard. Then run the following:

```
node index.js
```

Trigger a motion to capture the image. If the captured image matches one of the faces we indexed, we will not get an email; if it does, we will get an email.

Simple isn't it? This is a very powerful setup that we have built to provide surveillance at our homes or offices, where simple false alarms can be identified easily.

This example can be extended further to send push notifications or call neighbours using cloud-based calling services such as Twilio.

Summary

In this chapter, we have seen how to set up a smart surveillance system with Raspberry Pi and the AWS Rekognition platform.

We started by understanding the AWS Rekognition platform and then indexing/seeding a collection with our images. Next, we updated the Raspberry Pi code to take a picture when motion is detected and then send that image to AWS Rekognition to identify whether the face in the current photo matches any of the indexed images. If it does, we ignore the image; if it does not, we send an email with that image.

With this, we complete, *Practical Internet of Things with JavaScript*. I hope you have learned a few ways to leverage JavaScript and Raspberry Pi to build simple yet powerful IoT solutions.

Index

CPSIA information can be obtained
at www.ICGtesting.com
Printed in the USA
LVHW060120120820
662962LV00013B/2174